Healed and Transformed

A THERAPIST EXPLORES WHAT HAPPENED WHEN WOMEN MET JESUS

VICKI MULLINS EATON

Copyright © 2025 by Vicki Mullins Eaton

Published by Vicki Mullins Eaton Publishing

All rights reserved.

Cover design by Tommy Owen

All rights reserved. No part of this book may be reproduced in any form or by any electronic or mechanical means, including information storage and retrieval systems, without written permission from the author, except for the use of brief quotations in a book review.

The scanning, uploading, and distribution of this book without permission is a theft of the author's intellectual property. To obtain permission to quote from this book (other than for use of brief quotations in reviews), visit www.vickieatontherapy.com

Unless otherwise indicated, Scripture quotations are from THE HOLY BIBLE, NEW INTERNATIONAL VERSION®, NIV® Copyright © 1973, 1978, 1984, 2011 by Biblica, Inc.® Used by permission. All rights reserved worldwide.

Scripture quotations marked First Nations are from First Nations Version, An Indigenous Translation of the New Testament, published by InterVarsity Press and Rain Ministries, 2021.

Scripture quotations marked NRSV are from the New Revised Standard Version Bible, copyright © 1989 National Council of the Churches of Christ in the United States of America. Used by permission. All rights reserved worldwide.

Scripture quotations marked MSG are taken from *THE MESSAGE*, copyright © 1993, 2002, 2018 by Eugene H. Peterson. Used by permission of NavPress. All rights reserved. Represented by Tyndale House Publishers, Inc.

979-8-9939840-0-1

In memory of my sister, Brenda Mullins Lowe Petrey, who lived from April 17, 1953 to March 2, 2008. She brought so much beauty and love into this world and inspired me and many others.

Contents

Acknowledgments   7
Introduction   9

1. An Old Woman and a Young Woman   19
2. A Despairing Woman   35
3. A Scandalous Woman   49
4. A Despised Woman   67
5. A Discarded Woman   83
6. A Desperate Woman   99
7. Two Different Women   117
8. A Disregarded Woman   135

Resources   155
Notes   159

Acknowledgments

I'm so grateful for the people who gave me encouragement and/or feedback as I wrote this book, especially my husband Allen Eaton, my daughter Andrea Ensing, and my cousin, Cathy Carter Harden.

I'm also deeply grateful to the friends and colleagues who supported me emotionally and spiritually and gave me feedback about my writing:

- Janet Mullins
- Sheri Reeves
- Charlotte Parcels
- Mickey Kosman
- Mary Morgan
- Debbie Hervey
- Darlene Wildman
- Karyn Kim
- Wanda Morgan
- Kay Holler
- Brenda Moraine
- Grace Grammer
- Kathy Kearns Ross
- Dr. Christopher Mote.
- Sarah Tipton
- Writing coach, Keri Wyatt Kent
- The women of the Women's Ministry of the Vineyard Church, Gilbert, Arizona

Introduction

"All behavior serves a purpose."

There is an underlying reason why someone acts the way they do, even if their actions seem illogical or the consequences are harmful. Ever since I became a Social Worker and a therapist over thirty years ago, this statement—all behavior has a purpose—has been a lens that helps me see and understand better the people who work with me in therapy. It reminds me that sometimes people do things not because there is something wrong or bad about them but because they are simply trying to get a legitimate need met—like a need for love, approval, or significance—but they don't know how to do that in the healthiest way.

When I read the Bible, especially the stories in the four gospels—Matthew, Mark, Luke, and John—of women who met Jesus for the first time, that lens also helps me better understand them. Most of them were struggling emotionally, mentally, physically, spiritually, or socially when they first met Jesus. Some engaged in behaviors that put them in jeopardy or earned scorn from others. But Jesus didn't judge or reject them, which is what some of them received from the people around them. No, Jesus responded to each woman as though she was worthy of being seen and heard, accepted and loved. He treated them with respect and dignity.

Some of these women carried pain and heartache, experienced loneliness, felt like an outcast, grappled with loss, endured chronic illness and physical pain, felt insecurity and shame, and experienced anxiety and depression. Some knew what it was like to experience infertility or have a desperately ill child. Others had to deal with the pain of a spouse dying or divorcing them. Still others had to contend with the biases and prejudices of sexism, racism, and ageism.

Though these women lived in a different time, place, and culture than we live in today, at the core they were still women like you and me. They desired to have a life in which they felt safe, accepted, and valued. They longed to experience peace, love, and joy, but that was not the experience of many of them.

When they met Jesus, though, something dramatically changed in each of their lives. Their shame and depression lifted, their anxiety calmed down, their minds and bodies were healed. And they became free to embrace their truest identity as someone deeply loved and worthy. Because of an encounter with Jesus, each one experienced healing and transformation, and their lives were forever changed.

I began to realize these women have much to teach us about dealing with failure, fear, shame, sin, and experiencing forgiveness and love. They also show us what we can expect when we meet Jesus, invite him to reside within us, welcome him into all the rooms of our heart, including those where we carry pain and shame, and seek to walk with him daily.

My hope in writing this book is that more women will find increased healing and freedom than just those who sit and talk to me every week in my office. So, if you *know* you are deeply loved by God but you don't *feel* loved, this book is for you. If you feel stuck in feelings and behaviors that undermine you and you'd like to get unstuck, it's also for you. If you are aware of some lies you believe about yourself, others, or God, that get in the way of you moving forward in your life, this book could be for you, too.

Does any of this resonate with you? Like these women in the gospels, have you struggled with anything similar?

Reading about these women in the New Testament prompted me to reflect on some of the women I have worked with as a therapist through the years. Some began therapy simply looking for practical solutions for solving a problem, such as how to be a better parent to their toddler or teen, or how to more easily make the transition in a geographical move, or how to feel more confident on job interviews. Others wanted to process their grief about a major loss. Still others started therapy because they weren't happy and wanted freedom from the depression and sadness that colored their world in muted shades of gray. Some fought anxiety and were desperate to stop the panic that would rise up in them, sometimes interfering with even simple things, like making a phone call or going to the grocery store. Still others began therapy because they were trying to heal from the effects of trauma, whether it was a recent one, like a car accident, or an earlier trauma of growing up with abuse, neglect, or abandonment. Many of these women carried shame about their struggles and worried about what other people would think of them if they knew.

Though the women I worked with were different from each other in many ways, the one thing most of them had in common is that they had come to believe some things about themselves, about other people, and about God that may have *felt* true but, from God's perspective, were *not* true. In other words, they believed lies. Many of the lies were one (or more) of five common kinds of lies:

Possibility Lies: "I should have it all. I should be all. I should be able to do it all. I have to get as much out of every minute as possible."

Responsibility Lies: "I can't say no. It's up to me to be responsible for everyone and everything. It's not ok for me to have needs or wants. I can't let anyone down."

Capability Lies: "I'm not smart or competent enough. It's not ok to make mistakes. If I could just be smart (good, attractive, thin, etc.) enough, then I'd be ok."

Acceptability Lies: "I'm not worthy. I'm not acceptable. If anyone knew the real me, they'd reject me. I don't deserve good things."

Vulnerability Lies: "There is no safe place. I'm in danger. I can't let down my guard and trust anyone. I'm going to get hurt."

Do any of these lies feel true to you?

Some of the women who began therapy didn't realize they believed these lies, or they didn't understand the negative impact the lies had on them. They also didn't realize the lies they believed prompted them to either try too hard and do too much or try too little because they were afraid to step out in faith. Sometimes the lies they believed triggered a need to control everyone and everything and sometimes they triggered feelings of having no control.

Once they discovered how their lives were impacted by the lies they believed (and the past experiences that planted the lies in them), most women wanted to confront and refute what negative things felt true to them. Through therapy, scripture and Healing Prayer, many started on a journey with Jesus to become free of the lies that had held them back in life. When they were finally able to embrace the truth, "I am worthy of love, I'm loveable, and I'm deeply loved," and "I'm acceptable and accepted," they began to let go of the shame they carried. They began to live their lives more peacefully, lovingly, joyfully, purposefully, and yes, boldly. By reading this book, I believe you, also, can experience that same freedom.

Thinking about what women in the New Testament experienced also prompted me to reflect on my own life and the healing journey I've been on with Jesus that began in my young adult years and has continued through the decades of my life.

My healing journey began when I was four years old but, of course, I didn't know it at the time. I remember one Sunday morning my family and I were getting ready to go to church. I was dressed, ready to go, and was hanging out in the living room by myself as I listened to the sounds in the kitchen of my parents talking and laughing and dishes clattering in the sink as the breakfast table was cleared off. I recall Mom was relaxed and happy that day, so everything seemed bathed in sunshine.

I started thinking about the Sunday School class I would attend in a little while. In my child's mind I was trying to make sense of what was being taught but it was confusing. I wondered,

"If Jesus is God's son, why did he have to die on a cross?"

Suddenly I had an "aha" moment, and I was so excited to have figured it out.

"God loves us so much even though we are like"—and I tried to think of the most disgusting thing imaginable—"like a pile of vomit!" That's what my little four-year old mind thought.

Somehow at that young age I had already come to believe we were all so evil, dirty, and flawed in God's eyes, and yet Jesus loved us enough to pay the price for our sin. I was also learning there were a lot of rules I had to follow if I was to be acceptable to God. I heard God was a loving but angry and jealous God and that if I didn't say, "Yes," to him and follow his rules, I would go to Hell where there would be, "weeping, and wailing, and gnashing of teeth."

Now, *how* and *why* would a precious little girl have come to believe she was worth as much as a pile of vomit? What was being taught to me that I already knew those words?

The theology I was taught about God's tremendous love was correct but much of what I came to believe was reflective of the legalistic, shame-based home and church in which I grew up. "You should be ashamed of yourself." Those words I heard at home and church echoed in my mind as I, years later, explored the impact on my life of what I was taught as a child.

Two other factors reinforced that shame, and though they may seem trivial now, they had a huge influence on me. First, being the oldest of five kids in my family, and second, my experiences in school of being one of the youngest and smallest kids in my class prompted me to believe lies that affected how I lived my life for many years.

My mom had a medical condition that caused her to feel bad much of the time. My dad had a lot of responsibility at work and church, so he was always busy or tired from being so busy. As the oldest, caring for some of my younger siblings and helping with household chores fell to me. I was a pretty good kid, but my parents' emotional reactions were not always predictable. I came to believe some things that fell under the headings of "Responsibility Lies" and "Acceptability Lies."

In school I was one of the smallest and youngest kids in the class, was also a "late bloomer," and I had no older sibling to guide me. That essentially meant I was about two years emotionally and socially behind the girls in my class who had early birthdays, were "early bloomers," and who had older siblings from whom they could learn. All that fostered in me anxiety, self-doubt, insecurity, not knowing how to fit in, and a fear of being "just mediocre" or being a "nobody." Since I grew up in an era where corporal punishment was widely used, I also witnessed kids getting hit by teachers and principals, which also fueled my anxiety and fear. The things I came to believe from those experiences I later understood as "Capability Lies" and "Vulnerability Lies."

Putting all that together—home, church, and school—my identity eventually became one of someone who was good at being good. A rule follower. Mostly, a conformist. I have a memory in high school of not going to a Homecoming football game because it fell on a Friday night when our church was having a revival service. I received a lot of kudos for being such a "good and godly" kid when I was the only high school student at church that night. I didn't feel deprived at the time. Rather, I felt pride. Sadly, I also became someone who judged others who weren't rule-followers.

All that began to shift when I went to college and became active in a Christian ministry on campus. I was introduced to a different perspective of God, one who was much more merciful, grace giving, and loving than I'd previously learned. I was starting to internalize that love, when a big turning point for me came in my junior year. I was home on break and Dad and I went into a pharmacy together. Next to the entrance was a circular rack of books. His eyes and my eyes hit the same book at the same time. It was a book about how to like yourself. Dad scoffed and said, "That's what's wrong with this world. Too many people like themselves."

That was another big "aha" moment for me. I suddenly realized my dad believed if you liked yourself, it was pride, and pride was a sin. I don't recall ever having been told that specifically, but his statement matched something in me that felt true, that it was a sin to like yourself. Hearing his words triggered three things in me: First, a familiar sense of shame; second, a new realization that, "My dad doesn't really understand God's love;" and third, a huge revelation of...

"Oh, *this* is why I struggle with self-esteem and lack confidence."

And in that moment, I made a conscious decision that I was not only going to learn to love myself the way God loved me, but I was also going to learn to like myself. That decision started in earnest, a healing journey I had begun when I was four years old. I know now it's a journey that will continue until I cross over into heaven.

Fast forward a few years after college and I met my husband in seminary. We got married, graduated, and went into ministry together. Five years later we became parents of a baby boy we adopted from South Korea. Two more years and our baby girl was born. So, during those early years of parenthood I was a full-time, stay-at-home mom while my husband, Allen, was a pastor of a church. I call those years my "doing years" because along with caring for two active kids, I also volunteered *many* hours for our church and for my kids' school. There was a time when I was involved in five ministries at church and coordinated two of them as well as organized parent volunteers at my kids' school.

What was I thinking? What *lies* did I believe?

Fast forward a few more years and I went back to school and became a social worker and a therapist. I still stayed busy, though. One time when I was stretched beyond my limits of time and energy, someone came to me and said,

"Vicki, would you meet with me and my ministry team and let us pick your brain? You have such great ideas."

My mind and energy level said, "No, I can't take on another thing," but my mouth said, "Sure, I'll meet with your team."

Later that day I was upset with myself for saying I would help when my time and energy were already stretched so thin. I called out to God and implored him,

"Why do I keep doing this?"

Instantly I heard a voice in my head say, as clear as could be, "You love it when people think you are profound and so you take on things I never asked you to do."

Wow! As I contemplated what I had heard, I realized that even though I had already let go of a lot of the shame-based beliefs and lies I previously held, I still was trying to fill up something inside me that was determined to *not* be a nobody, to *not* be just mediocre. I felt ashamed but when I brought it before God, His truth suddenly washed over me, reminding me that I already *am* somebody—somebody designed in an amazing way, incredibly cherished and loved, worthy of being held and comforted by Him like a little child needing nurture, and someone who doesn't have to keep *doing, doing, doing* to be acceptable and accepted.

I'm still discovering how okay it is to just *be*. *Be* with God. *Be* with others. And *be* with myself. These are lessons I continue to learn, and they are ones I believe can help you as well.

You don't have to have been abused as a child or betrayed by someone you loved to have come to believe lies about yourself, others, or God. In fact, it's rather common. The only people I've met who can more closely and consistently live out of God's truth about themselves are people who have faced the pain in their life, let go of the lies that feel true, who have encountered Jesus in a deep way, and who continue to seek God's presence daily.

I'm so glad you decided to read this book. It is my hope that exploring what happened to these women when they met Jesus will help you come to *see* yourself as loved, *believe* you are loved, and *feel* loved the same way Jesus sees and loves you. May your journey through this study either start you on the road to healing or help you further the process you've already begun.

ONE

An Old Woman and a Young Woman

LUKE 2:21-28

AT A BUSY GROCERY STORE, I waited in a long line at the check-out counter. I noticed two other customers: an older woman alone and a young woman carrying a tiny baby. It occurred to me they were at opposite ends of adult life, one at the beginning and one at the end.

As the older woman slowly loaded her groceries onto the conveyor belt, it was clear she was struggling and the adventure called life was winding down for her. I wondered, "What experiences did she have, joyful and painful, that brought her to this point? Does she struggle financially or have medical concerns? Are her family and friends still living or is she alone? Has she lived her best life, or does she have a lot of regrets?"

Behind her, the young woman "wearing her baby" in a carrier against her chest swayed gently, whispering soothing words to her baby. I wondered, "How is she adjusting to being a new mom? Does she have someone supportive and helpful in her life, or is she parenting alone? Did she receive the kind of mothering that will either help or hinder her in being the mom her baby needs?"

These two women give us a glimpse of what two other

women, one at the beginning and one at the end of adulthood, might have been experiencing in the first century as introduced to us in Luke.

THE STORY

Anna was only married for seven years before she became a widow. No doubt, the death of her husband dramatically altered the course of her life. When our story takes place, she is eighty-four years old. Whatever hopes and dreams she had as a young woman were long over. During those seven years of marriage how she pictured her life as an old woman was probably quite different than how it turned out.

We don't know what happened to her in the intervening years. Besides grieving a huge loss, Anna possibly had to contend with a lack of options for caring for her needs. Widows in the culture of that day could return to their father's house if he were still alive, live with an adult son, or marry a brother-in-law. If none of those options were available, she could have difficulty providing for her own basic needs. Since poverty was common and women were not permitted to inherit money from a husband or a father, it could be devastating to a widow. Some had to resort to begging to even have food to eat. We don't know if any of this happened to Anna, but here is what we do know:

When our story takes place, Anna had chosen a nontraditional option. Her deep, personal faith in the God of Abraham, Isacc, and Jacob is likely what got her through her pain. This godly woman dedicated her life to continual prayer, worship of God, and fasting, and she never left the temple grounds. We don't know if she lived in the temple all those years or if she had other options as a young widow.

By the time this story took place, Anna was believed to be a prophetess. When God's Spirit prompted her, she occasionally preached to the crowds or shared a prophetic word with someone who visited the temple. Interestingly, it was believed women were so unreliable they were not permitted to testify in court, yet Anna was known as credible and reliable by women and probably many men, also.

Anna was present the day a young couple named Mary and Joseph brought their eight-day old baby boy to the temple for the first time. In much of today's world Mary would be seen as too young to be a mother, since it's assumed she was somewhere between fifteen and sixteen years old when she delivered her baby. But she was viewed as an adult back then.

When God chose to come to earth as a baby, He picked Mary to be the mother. Now, you would think everything would go smoothly for anyone chosen for such an important assignment, and you might expect someone to feel at peace after hearing a message from an angel, but the appearance of the angel both jarred and perplexed Mary.

"Do not be afraid, Mary, for you have found favor with God. And now you will conceive in your womb and bear a son, and you will name him Jesus. He will be great, and will be called the Son of the Most High, and the Lord God will give to him the throne of his ancestor, David. He will reign over the House of Jacob forever, and of his kingdom there will be no end." (Luke 1:26-33, NRSV)

Mary's response was, "Here am I, the servant of the Lord. Let it be with me according to your word." (Luke 1:38, NRSV)

What an incredible honor to be chosen for such a task! But after the angel left and she calmed down, the reality of her situation probably set in. Mary knew if a young woman got pregnant without being married, she could be stoned to death. Who would believe her when the baby bump began to show, and she tried to explain, "Believe me, I'm carrying the Messiah. It's totally a miracle!" She also probably worried, wondering: "How will I break the news to my parents and to Joseph?

What will my friends think? If I'm not stoned, will I be shunned?"

We don't know how her parents responded, but when she first told Joseph about her pregnancy, he assumed she had been unfaithful to him. He decided to quietly end their relationship. This likely grieved her in two ways. First, that he would believe something like that about her, and second, that God's plan was going to cause her to lose the love of her life. Those concerns likely prompted her to leave home and travel to the Judean hills near Jerusalem to stay with her cousin Elizabeth for a while. Mary must have felt so relieved, though, when Joseph told her an angel had appeared to him and assured him that she had told the truth and that he should marry her.

When our story picks up, this drama has subsided, the new mother has given birth, and the baby is now eight days old. The young family set off from Bethlehem to Jerusalem, about six miles away, to complete the first ritual required by their Jewish faith: Consecrate their first-born baby boy to God through circumcision and give him his official name, Yeshua in Hebrew, or Jesus in English.

What a momentous occasion! When this young couple arrived at the temple, they were just two excited new parents who wanted to do what was required by their faith. They'd already fallen in love with this baby and were in awe that God would entrust this little one to them to parent. They also likely had similar anxiety and insecurity that many new parents often experience. Perhaps they wondered:

"What if he gets hungry while we are there? What if he starts crying? Are we bringing enough swaddling clothes for when he needs to be changed?"

If you have ever welcomed a new baby into your family, do you remember what it was like the first time you took him or her to a family gathering or church? You and the baby probably received much attention, questions, and advice. That may have happened to Mary and Joseph. As they made their way through the crowd, I wonder how many people stopped to congratulate them and admire the baby?

Perhaps they heard expressions like, "Oh, he is so cute!" "He looks like he has his Mama's eyes." "How is he sleeping?" "Are *you* getting any sleep?" "Becoming a parent totally changes your life, doesn't it?"

No doubt, Anna would have known Simeon, a devout older man who also worshiped at the temple daily. When Mary and Joseph arrived at the temple, Simeon instantly recognized *this* baby was the one he had been waiting for, and the one Israel had been anticipating for over four hundred years. *This* baby was Christ, the promised Messiah! Simeon took Baby Jesus in his arms, offered praise to God and a prophecy to his parents about Jesus:

"This child is destined to cause the falling and rising of many in Israel, and to be a sign that will be spoken against, so the thoughts of many hearts will be revealed." (Luke 2:34).

And then he told Mary, "A sword will pierce your own soul too" (Luke 2:35). What strange words for new parents to hear! The incongruity of a blessing and the disconcerting words may have brought a sense of unreality to that moment.

Anna arrived at the scene just then and wholeheartedly agreed with Simeon's words. As she expressed thanks to God for this baby, she turned to the crowd around them and testified about the meaning of this baby's birth.

Perhaps that day at the temple, Anna's and Simeon's words revived hope that Israel was about to enter a new era and be released from sixty-three years of Roman oppression prior to Jesus' birth.[1]

Anna and Mary, two women with different experiences in life and whose lives intersected for only a moment in time, have valuable things to teach us. If we explored all the possibilities, it would become a book so in this one chapter we will concentrate on three things they had in common as they experienced healing and transformation.

Anna and Mary both experienced pain and trauma and felt anxious and afraid at times, but God healed their pain and transformed their lives.

When Anna's husband died, she experienced grief complicated by stress from whatever options she had as a widow. She may have believed things that *felt* true, but from God's perspective were lies, "I'm all alone. I can't take care of myself. I'm homeless." She probably believed things that fell under the headings of "capability lies" and "vulnerability lies." We don't know how long her grief lasted or anything else about her life until we meet her in the second chapter of Luke. We know eventually she realized God was powerful and loved her enough to fill up the empty, lonely places inside her. She did not allow her pain and grief to define her. She gave God permission to use it for good in her life and in service to others. It likely took her some time to get to that point emotionally and spiritually but eventually she was able to affirm the truth of, "I'm not alone. I'm well cared for. I live where I am safe and significant."

Mary also experienced fear and trauma in her life as the mother of Jesus. Perhaps Simeon's words, "A sword will pierce your soul," helped fuel her fear. Two incidents stand out:

One night she was awakened by Joseph. "Mary, get up! An angel came to me in a dream and said Herod is going to search for our baby and kill him. We need to get out of here as quickly as possible and cross the border into Egypt." (Matthew 2:13-15, NRSV)

Mary *believed* God the Father would protect and help them escape, but it's not likely she *felt* calm and peaceful. The "fight, flight, or freeze" response[2] programmed by God into all of us that automatically gets activated when we believe we are in danger probably instantly kicked in for Mary. In her mind she could affirm God was in control, but what lies probably *felt* true in that moment were:

"Oh, no, my baby is going to die. This is the moment that a sword is going to pierce my soul."

Mary believed some lies that fell under the heading of "Vulnerability Lies." Not until they crossed the border into another country was she able to let go, breathe deeply, and say, "Okay, we're safe now. My baby is safe." Of course, Mary couldn't see the army of angels around them every step of the way, but once they were safe, she was probably able to relax and acknowledge that Herod's soldiers would never have been able to penetrate the angelic shield around them.

Another time Mary became afraid was when the family made their annual pilgrimage to the temple in Jerusalem. At the end of their first homeward bound day, Mary and Joseph discovered twelve-year-old Jesus was not with the group. She immediately started to worry. Perhaps she believed, "Oh, no! My son is gone. This is it...*this* is where a sword will pierce my soul." The parents frantically returned to Jerusalem in search of Jesus. What a relief to finally discover him safe in the temple conversing with the teachers. Perhaps this experience gave Mary an opportunity to practice something she would eventually have to do: let go of her son and give him to God the Father. Having no idea what form "the sword" would take or when it would happen likely made it even more difficult to release him.

Both Anna and Mary eventually came to understand that their minute-by-minute walk with God allowed them to heal from the pain of trauma, be freer of anxiety, and focus on the future with hope and peace.

Both women said, "Yes," to God even though what they were invited to do was hard and heart breaking.

If Anna had the opportunity to choose the life she preferred, it wouldn't have been the one she had, at least not at first. The pain from the death of her husband was difficult enough but if she also had to be concerned about food and shelter, that multiplied her pain. Of course, this was not something to which she wanted to say, "yes."

But she didn't have a choice. This was what life thrust upon her. Did her trust in God's care come quickly and easily? Or was it developed the same way a muscle gets bigger, stronger, and more defined—by being challenged with increased weight? Since the text tells us Anna spent her days praying, I wonder if her belief in God's dependability developed over time through prayers such as,

"God, I believe you are real, that you are good, and that you will take care of me. Please give me the strength to get through this. Thank you for providing what I needed today."

Anna didn't know her "yes" to God in the middle of her pain and fear would lead to the biggest adventure of her life: being a member of the welcome team for baby Jesus and preparing the hearts of people for Messiah's arrival.

Mary also said, "yes," to something hard. Think about it. As a mother, if you had been told something would eventually happen to your baby that would "put a sword through your soul," wouldn't those words whisper in your mind and trigger anxiety occasionally? For years she had to live with the unknowing, the uncertainty about what was going to happen in her son's life to fulfill Simeon's prophecy. Mary had to learn one of the hardest lessons a parent must learn – how to let go and trust God to care for and protect her child when she wasn't there.

As Jesus became an adult and began to travel around the country to teach about God's kingdom, perhaps it was easy at first to think, "Ok, this is good. People love my son. Maybe Simeon was wrong."

But when it became clear the religious leaders were increasingly unhappy with her son, her anxiety probably ramped up again. And then in those last few days of Jesus' life as she watched him get arrested, sentenced to death, and take his last breath on that terrible cross, there was nothing else she could do except, in her agony, let go and trust God would care for him as he hung on that cross and beyond. Mary's "yes" to God's plan was excruciatingly hard, but she did it.

Anna and Mary both lived out their life's purpose.

After her husband died, there were likely times when Anna

questioned what she was supposed to do with her life, something many women question when they become a widow. For a while she may have believed "capability lies" of "I can't do this. I don't have what it takes. I'm alone and I can't take care of myself." She likely did not immediately jump into habits of continual prayer and worship and fasting. At first it may have been out of desperation. As she found comfort in them, though, she discovered she was drawn to a prayerful and meditative lifestyle. Eventually she no longer did them just for comfort but because she realized God was doing something within her: healing and transforming her pain. And He was doing something through her: ministering to others. By that time in her life, she probably wouldn't have changed anything about it.

Isn't it interesting God used her deepest pain to introduce Anna to her calling—her *why* for being on earth at that time in history. Like John the Baptizer, she became one of those who prepared the way for Jesus to enter human history as he ushered in his kingdom. That day in the temple represented the culmination of Anna's life's purpose as she met an eight-day old baby boy. Perhaps, she knew it was finished, that she had lived out her purpose and could now return Home.

It's not difficult to figure out Mary's life's purpose. God specifically chose her to be Jesus' mom. He knew Jesus would receive the kind of parenting that would facilitate a secure and healthy attachment between mother and baby. How delighted Mary must have been as she watched this little guy do all the cute things babies do as they learn to sit up, stand, walk, run, climb, talk, explore, learn how to learn, and fall peacefully asleep against her chest while being rocked. As a mom she must have been so proud to watch him grow into being a kind, trustworthy, honest, smart, and brave young man.

God knew Mary's mothering of Jesus would be part of the strength he needed to grow into being a man strong enough to stand up to bullies and gentle enough to hold and bless a young child. He also knew that no matter how anxious Mary became, she would always encourage Jesus to follow God, even if it led to a cross. There were probably other moments when Mary asked herself, "Is today the day a sword will pierce my soul?" Perhaps those thoughts even became a steady rhythm in her mind as the religious leaders' hostility towards him grew.

And then one day she knew. She finally had to say, "Yes, today is the day."

WHAT CAN WE LEARN FROM ANNA AND MARY'S STORIES?

Anna and Mary both experienced painful trauma in their lives. All of us have experienced trauma and pain in our lives, also, and have felt anxious and afraid. But God wants to heal our pain and transform our lives.

I've not heard anyone say, "I've never experienced pain or trauma." It's part of living in a pain-filled world where sin exists, where hurtful things happen to each of us, and where we have also caused pain in someone's life on occasion.

What happened in your life that caused you sadness, anxiety, shame, or anger?

Allowing yourself to grieve and feel the feelings associated with painful experiences are important steps toward the healing and transformation God wants to do in your life. You can ignore or mute your pain, but it only causes it to go underground in your heart, mind, and body, and come out in unhealthy ways. Yet many of us in the church are afraid to openly admit our pain. We fear being judged and many have experienced that.

Have you ever shared your pain but another Christian either dismissed, judged, or tried to fix you? Is it easier to just smile, put

*on a "church face," and pretend everything is good when
everything is churning underneath?*

That's not what God wants for you. You weren't meant to hide and pretend. God wants to shine His light into any dark and lonely place in your heart and mind and to bring His love, truth, and peace into those memories where the lies formed. He wants to set you free from the power the lies have held over you so His Spirit can more easily flow through you and bring love and light into a world deeply in need of that.

Have you ever visited a garden and noticed the richness of the soil? If so, it's probably one where the gardener uses composted soil. A garden where things get composted illustrates what God wants to do with your pain.

Compost is soil that comes from plant-based waste products, such as dead leaves, grass clippings, banana and potato peels, and coffee grounds. If you live near a farm that raises cows, horses, or chickens—any plant-eating animal—you can add manure to the compost pile. What is being composted must be thoroughly watered and then turned every day. It begins to heat up from the inside which kills the weed seeds. Eventually it breaks down into rich soil in which nutritious, delicious, and beautiful foods and flowers abundantly grow. Composted soil becomes what gardeners call "black gold."

And God is in the composting business. He takes the "shittiest" experiences in our lives, thoroughly waters them with our tears, and painstakingly turns them over and over. Eventually, it breaks down into "black gold," something from which beautiful things can grow. Any follower of Jesus who has gone through difficulties, will discover that God wants to "compost" those difficulties so something good will grow from them. Sometimes what grows is greater wisdom and compassion but sometimes it's an ability to walk beside someone going through a similar difficulty, helping them to heal.

What needs to be composted in your life?

Just like God asked Anna and Mary to do something hard and heart breaking, sometimes God asks us to do things that are hard, that potentially break our heart.

"I Never Promised You a Rose Garden" is a country music song recorded back in 1970 by Lynn Anderson. There was also a book by that title published many years ago. That phrase has come to be synonymous with the idea that perfection in life is not promised to us and that we all must deal with difficult things sometimes. Perhaps that analogy developed because, while roses are beautiful and smell sweet, they also have thorns.

There are many "thorny" things we would never choose to experience if it was up to us, like the death of a loved one, a cancer diagnosis, being severely injured in an accident, or unemployment. Most of the time, though, we don't get a choice. The question then becomes,

"What do we do when we are faced with something hard or heart breaking?"

A full answer to that would go *way* beyond the small space allotted here, so I will just point out what Anna and Mary did:

They both said, "yes." Not quickly. Not easily. But eventually that was how they responded to what life threw at them.

What might God be asking you to say "yes" to in your life that's hard or even heart-breaking?

Just like God had a reason for Anna's and Mary's lives, we are also here on earth at this time in history for a reason.

"You have a purpose in life." Not exactly a new idea. You've probably heard that many times, but do you know what it means for you specifically?

Your first reason for being here is to learn to love...love God, love others including your enemies, and yes, love yourself the way God loves you. Your second reason for being here is that you have a "calling" to do something specific, something that resonates strongly within you. Once you understand it, you orient your life around it. You were designed by God for it, and God wants to empower you to do it.

"It's in Christ that we find out who we are and what we are living for. Long before we first heard of Christ and got our hopes up, he had his eyes on us, had designs on us for glorious living, part of the overall purpose he is working out in everything and everyone." (Ephesians 1:11, MSG).

Here are some clues that help you figure out your life's purpose: what you love and are passionate about, your inborn temperament, the strengths and talents you have, what you value most, your hopes and dreams, the wonderful and, yes, even the painful experiences in your life, feedback from a trusted believer about what they see in you, and scripture.

Do you know your life's purpose? On a scale of 1-10, if 10 is, "I know what my life's purpose is and I fully live it out," and 5 is, "I know what my life's purpose is but I don't really live it out," and 0 is, "I don't have a clue what my life's purpose is," where are you on that 0-10 scale now?

When you figure out your life's purpose, or what God is calling you to, then live it out. You will experience a greater sense of meaning, joy, and adventure in your life. It will also allow you at the end of your life, like Anna, to be able to say, "I lived my life according to God's plan for it. I learned the lessons I was supposed to learn here, and now I'm ready to go Home."

PRAYER

Lord Jesus, as we begin this study of women who were healed and transformed by an encounter with you, we invite you to go on that same journey with each of us. You intimately know the amazing ways we were designed by Creator God, as well as what painful experiences we've had that interfere with us fully embracing our truest identity as your precious daughter.

You not only know what traumas we experienced in life, you also know how scary or uncomfortable it can feel to recall those memories. So, if something in this book brings up painful memories, please remind us we are not alone now. Hold our hand as you lovingly and gently shine your light into any memories where hurt, shame, fear, or anger remain. Show us what lies got installed in those memories. Set us free from the power of the lies. And plant your truth in every part of our mind and body about who we really are in your eyes.

For any woman who currently faces a difficult situation she doesn't want and didn't choose, please provide what she needs in a concrete, tangible way. Allow her to experience your presence surrounding her, covering her, lifting her up, and holding her. Let her experience your tender care in whatever way she most needs to receive it as she moves toward being able to say, "Yes."

God, we know you had a picture of each woman in your mind and a plan for her life before she was ever conceived. Please bring clarity to her about her *why*, her life's purpose. Then empower her with your Spirit to live the life you call her to, and please, turn all of it into a great adventure.

Lord, thank you in advance for bringing further healing and transformation into each woman's life.

In Jesus Christ's name, amen.

QUESTIONS FOR PERSONAL REFLECTION AND GROUP SHARING

1. In what ways do you identify either with Anna or Mary?

2. What emotional, mental, physical, or spiritual pain or trauma are you currently experiencing or have experienced in your life?
3. Which lies get triggered most in your life, *Possibility, Responsibility, Capability, Acceptability*, or *Vulnerability Lies*?
4. What still needs to be "composted" in your life?
5. What is something you have had to say, "yes," to that's hard or heart-breaking, and how has it impacted your life?
6. What do you know about your life's purpose?

AN EXERCISE TO TRY: LISTENING

Anna spent much of her life in prayer, talking to God and listening for His voice. If you are like me, talking to God is much easier than stopping all the activity and just listening. Anna truly understood the scripture, "Be still and know I am God." (Psalm 46:10). Being still can feel uncomfortable, though.

Would you be willing to experiment with silence? Find a quiet place and turn off your phone. It's not a time to accomplish anything but a time for doing *nothing* except listening.

Invite God's Spirit to be present with you and to speak into your heart and mind, and then just listen. You might hear nothing but notice what happens. Maybe something will come to your mind, a person, picture, thought, song, scripture, movie, memory that you might not have been thinking about initially. Just notice.

It's also likely your mind will bring thoughts of what you should be doing and other physical distractions. Remind yourself this is simply a time of doing nothing except listening and readying your mind to hear God speak. The first time I tried this exercise, I noticed I felt hungry, started craving vanilla ice cream, and had to keep bringing my attention back to just listening. And that was all in the first minute and ten seconds.

You might experience something right away or you might not at all, but don't give up trying. It is a way of developing pathways in your brain associated with listening for God's voice, and soon you will hear it more.

TWO
A Despairing Woman
MARK 5:21-34

Miss Willy, a "guard dog," had been chained up outside her owner's house for twelve years, with only a dilapidated doghouse to protect her from temperamental weather. The amount of freedom she had ended with the length of her chain. She never received belly rubs, car rides, nor played "fetch." She lived her entire life alone and lonely without attention or love, except occasionally someone from a dog rescue organization checked on her. Her owner repeatedly refused to give her up. Miss Willy never received healthcare, either, so when she became so weak from an advanced case of heart worm that she could hardly stand, her owner finally agreed to relinquish her. Her rescuer was determined to make the rest of her life as enjoyable and comfortable as possible. So, for the last sixteen days of her life, she slept in a comfy dog bed inside, received lots of belly rubs and ear scratches, went on car rides to the beach, and even had a birthday party. Someone cared enough about her to set her free from the chains that held her captive for twelve long years.

In the gospel of Mark, we read a story about a despairing woman who was also set free from the chains that held her captive for twelve long years.

THE STORY

"Please come to my home," begged an anguished father as he knelt at Jesus' feet. "My little girl is dying. Please come and put your hands on her so she will be healed and live." (Mark 5:23) With that, Jesus began to follow the man towards his home.

Movement was slow, though, as a crowd of people surrounded Jesus, all trying to get a front row seat to witness the miraculous things he did. Suddenly, in the midst of the chaos, Jesus stopped. He'd felt his power flow out to someone in the crowd.

Jesus could've said, "Great, someone received healing," and kept going. After all, the man who begged Jesus to come was in a life-or-death situation. Jesus' healing powers were needed quickly. As a religious leader of the local synagogue, this man also could've been an ally for Jesus at a time when other religious leaders were starting to view him suspiciously. It might have been politically wise for Jesus to keep going, but he did not. He knew someone had sought healing from him and it would not be complete if it was not publicly acknowledged.

So, he stopped in the middle of his rush to save a little girl's life. Despite a loving father's fear and angst, Jesus stopped to release a woman from the chains that had kept her a prisoner for twelve years.

"Who touched my clothes?" (vs. 30) Jesus asked.

"Really? Look around. There are lots of people here pushing to see you. You've probably been touched by many," the disciples said as they probably rolled their eyes. Maybe they thought, "Come on, Dude, now is your chance to gain an ally. Some leaders aren't happy with you. You need this guy on your side. Don't blow this chance by stopping now."

Still, Jesus stopped.

A woman who despaired of ever being healed was so tired of it all—the pain, shame, and loneliness. She heard Jesus was traveling nearby, and no doubt, his reputation for miraculously healing people sparked a glimmer of hope within her. She was determined to get close to him even though, according to religious law, she really wasn't supposed to be in a crowd. She had done what was expected of her and carefully avoided people for twelve years. The last thing she wanted was attention. She wanted to quietly get close to Jesus, unobtrusively touch the hem of his coat, and quickly slip away. As he scanned the crowd and asked that question, she knew she couldn't hide. She wanted to acknowledge she felt something healed in her body, but the crowd would have still seen her as unclean. So, she fearfully came forward and admitted what she had done.

What was her story and why would she want to be inconspicuous?

For twelve long years, this woman endured a continual menstrual period. Unlike the usual three to seven days a month most women experience, her period never stopped. This meant she was classified as unclean and untouchable by Jewish law at that time, so everyone avoided her. If she was not married, she wouldn't have been allowed to get married. If she was married the law would have prohibited her from sex with her husband which would have been grounds for divorce. That means she might have been homeless by the time she met Jesus.

She was desperate to heal and had spent much money on remedies from doctors, but none had helped her. In fact, she was worse off. Today, we understand possible medical conditions that would cause continual menstrual bleeding: Hormonal imbalances between estrogen and progesterone; Uterine fibroids or polyps; Endometriosis; and bleeding disorders.

For example, a young woman in Australia started having periods at age 14. Her bleeding continued for five years until she was finally diagnosed with Von Willebrand's Disease, a blood clotting disorder.[1] Instead of losing the usual 20 - 60 milliliters of blood many women lose over a four-day period, she lost about 500 milliliters. She often fainted, had low blood pressure, and became seriously anemic, even with weekly transfusions of iron. She finally experienced relief when she was prescribed a blood product that is given to men with Hemophilia. This treatment finally allowed her to actively engage in life again.

Perhaps this poor woman in Mark who sought healing from Jesus experienced one of these disorders. But in the first century, no one knew why this woman bled. They assumed she was being punished for her sin.

In addition to physical symptoms perhaps she experienced the emotional distress many women feel before and during their period. Do you ever experience "ups and downs" emotionally at that time during your cycle? Many women report an increase in feelings of sadness, insecurity, anxiety, and irritability right before or during their period. Several women I've worked with in therapy felt so depressed during that time of the month that they admitted to feeling suicidal even though they assured me they would never follow through on it. Maybe this woman who sought healing from Jesus regularly experienced that kind of emotional instability.

Imagine what it would have been like to experience twelve years of bleeding at a time when there were no tampons or pads. And think about the cramping, bloating, irregular sleep, and the general physical discomfort she may have endured.

The worst part of it, though, may have been the social isolation and being excluded because she was "unclean" according to Jewish law. That meant everything she touched was seen as unclean, and everyone who touched her or touched anything she touched also became unclean. She was not allowed to go to the Temple and worship. She was likely not welcome in the marketplace. Nor could she engage in the traditional kiss of greeting, much like our tradition of shaking hands, when she encountered someone she knew. Hospitality was central to their culture, but no one would've come to her home if she still had one, nor would anyone invite her to theirs. No hugs. No hand holding. Imagine how lonely, depressed, and ashamed she must have felt after twelve years of such isolation. She had been mandated to be alone, so people avoided her "like the plague."

Being judged as evil and a sinner because of a medical problem was the ultimate humiliation. Of course, she wanted to stay hidden when she touched the hem of Jesus' coat. What a presumptuous thing for her to do! How unpopular that would have been to be discovered at the center of a crowd. Anyone she touched, including Jesus, could become "unclean" if she intentionally or accidentally touched them.

According to the Jewish laws of that day, several factors contributed to something being identified as unclean: skin diseases (such as Leprosy or Psoriasis), genital discharges (semen or blood), touching something dead, eating certain foods considered to be unclean (such as pork and shellfish), or touching anyone or anything in a state of uncleanness.[2] A woman who gave birth was considered unclean for eight days and not allowed to worship at the Temple for 40 days if her baby was a boy, simply because of the normal blood flow after childbirth. If her baby was a girl, however, she was considered unclean for fourteen days and barred from worship for eighty days.[3]

How inconvenient to touch something or someone considered unclean. Certain rituals had to be completed to be clean again, including taking a bath, washing your clothes, and waiting until evening arrived. Having no laundry facility and no shower made becoming clean considerably more difficult then than it would be today. No wonder people didn't want her to get near them. And how incredibly discouraged she must have been by the time this story took place.

It's understandable this woman was so desperate she willingly risked the wrath of the crowd and Jesus to touch the hem of his coat. Perhaps she thought because there were so many people he would never notice. No wonder she was fearful when he said, "Who touched me?" She knew she *had* done something wrong and broken the law. Now she had been found out and she didn't know what either Jesus or the crowd would do. She was fearful of the rebuke she believed would come.

But Jesus did not rebuke her.

Jesus was not offended she'd touched him. He instantly had compassion for the suffering she endured during those twelve years of, essentially, being in chains. Jesus knew the physical problem she experienced was only part of what needed to be healed. She also needed to be healed from the wounds caused by lies she had come to believe about herself and her worth: "I'm defective. I'm bad. I'm unworthy. I sinned and so I don't deserve to be loved." She may have come to believe lies about the people around her as well. Things like: "No one cares about me. I'm not wanted by anyone. I am nothing to them." And finally, she likely believed lies about God: "God is against me. He is not for me. God cares for others but not for me. God is mad at me and is punishing me. I can never do enough to be healed or cared for by God." She probably had embraced a long list of *Acceptability Lies.*

As a therapist who is also a follower of Jesus, I believe Jesus knew simply healing her physically would not be enough. Her healing needed to go to a deeper level to become free of the lies that had become her emotional identity because of the trauma of those twelve years. Jesus also knew that part of her healing meant she needed to come out into the open where she could be seen, heard, and touched by others. He knew doing so would break the chains of shame, hiding and avoiding others. He knew his healing love needed to reach into her heart and mind as well as her womb.

She knew instantly something had healed within as soon as she touched the hem of his coat, but when he said those incredible words,

"Daughter, your faith has made you well. Go in peace and be freed from your suffering," (vs.34) her whole identity immediately shifted. No longer a prisoner in a broken body. No longer an outcast. She no longer had to keep to herself to avoid causing someone else to become unclean. No more hiding in the shadows. She was finally free of the chains she had been in for twelve years. What relief, joy and gratitude she must have felt!

I wonder who she hugged first?

WHAT CAN WE LEARN FROM THIS WOMAN'S STORY?

As I read this story, I learn something different when I approach it first, as a social worker, second, as a therapist, and third, as a child of God. Each perspective offers different information.

First, as a Social Worker, I'm aware this woman had a disease considered incurable.

Today it's known as chronic, or "long illness," an illness that doesn't heal easily and sometimes doesn't even improve with a regularly prescribed solution. It might linger for months or even years and you may vacillate between feeling better and worse. There are many such illnesses as "long Covid," lupus, Alzheimer's, rheumatoid arthritis, epilepsy, and diabetes, to name a few.

According to the Center for Disease Control (CDC) it's estimated about 129 million people in the United States have at least one long or chronic illness.[4] Globally, it's estimated that one in three adults have multiple chronic illnesses, and that is expected to rise.

These kinds of illnesses can be exceedingly difficult to live with and treat. Here's how they can impact your life:

- Energy levels are unpredictable. One day you may have energy to do your job and the next you may feel so exhausted you can't get out of bed.

- Constant pain, dizziness, nausea, headaches, digestive upsets, and other physical symptoms that can come and go.
- Depression: belief that things aren't getting better and worry they never will.
- Anxiety about doctor's visits, tests, painful procedures, and hospitalizations.
- Lack of understanding and empathy from others can happen as you may *appear* well, and tests are initially inconclusive. That can result in judgments of, "Maybe it's all in your head," or "Just talk more positively to yourself," or "Pray more."

Sadly, I've heard many stories of people who have visited numerous doctors and gone through many tests with inconclusive results, sometimes for years. Hearing this woman's story from the perspective of a social worker I would ask questions like,

What conditions do you have that embarrass you or make you feel self-conscious? Defective? If you experience any kind of long illness, how does it affect your life and your family's life? What practical help do you need?

I would also likely offer a referral to a Functional Medicine doctor and an Acupuncturist.

Second, from the perspective of a therapist, I can assume this woman experienced emotions that commonly accompany a long illness:

They feel grief and loss that their life has dramatically changed, and they don't seem to have any power and control over that. There might be anger and frustration with themselves for not being able to rise above it and live their life as desired.

Perhaps hopelessness has taken up residence in them as they go to doctor after doctor, try a variety of medications, procedures and even supplements, but nothing helps ease their suffering.

There may be layers of trauma from the numerous doctors' visits, tests, painful procedures, hospitalizations, and constant pain. These experiences can result in Post Traumatic Stress Disorder, which can occur after being exposed to a single event or a series of events that was extremely overwhelming.[5] There is no doubt this woman was traumatized by all she endured for those twelve years, and she finally despaired of becoming healthy again. But she did not have a one-time trauma event. She had a history of trauma and the effects of it accumulated through those twelve years. That's the thing about trauma. It gets tattooed on your mind and body and eventually, if you ignore or push it down, it will gain power and come out in other ways physically, mentally, or emotionally.

Sometimes Christians believe that we just need to cling to God, read our Bible, and pray more. Those things can certainly help change the effects of trauma, but God has also designed our bodies to react to trauma in specific ways: fight, flight, or freeze.[6] Each way can help us if something dangerous is happening. But the solution is not always that simple. Sometimes, the mind and body can *get stuck* in fight, flight or freeze mode and is not able to shut off that response to it. That's what Post Traumatic Stress Disorder does, and then every time you either remember in your mind what happened, or you encounter something that reminds you of the trauma, it activates that response along with the many physical and emotional symptoms that accompany it.

Feeling alone, isolated, and embarrassed is common. It may seem no one really understands what is happening. Sometimes people even stop asking, "How are you today?"

Shame may be strongly connected to the lies you believe about yourself, others, and God, because of what you are experiencing.

There is a saying among some counselors that, "Secrecy maintains shame." It can be very freeing to "come out of the shadows" and share with another person something you have felt shame and embarrassment about, and then to receive their acceptance and support. What a blessing it can be to be part of a church or small group that offers a place where people can heal without fear of being judged or rejected.

Thinking about the lies this woman believed, what lies feel true to you today about yourself, others, and God, even if you logically know they are not true?

Third, as I read this story from the perspective of being a precious child of God, I noticed Jesus responded to her in a way that changed her whole identity.

He made time for her. She wasn't just an interruption to something important he was doing. He stopped and he really saw and heard her. He recognized she was a real person, but someone who lived in the shadows. In that instant he understood the ways she had been excluded from society.

He immediately was attuned to the pain she was in and the suffering and humiliation she had endured for twelve years. He expressed no judgement or rejection. He didn't give her advice on what she should change in her life. He had nothing but compassion and kindness for her. Jesus also was simply present with her in her pain but even more, he called her, "Daughter." This woman was the only person recorded in scripture that Jesus ever called "daughter."

Think about the significance of that. It meant she was no longer an outcast. He welcomed her back into her family, community, and the family of God. She was free to take her place again in society. And she was able to step into her truest identity of being a welcomed, precious daughter of Father God and a child of the King.

This is what Jesus wants to happen for each of us as women—to flood our heart, mind, and body with his love, peace, and truth. That is what he wants to bring right into the middle of those trauma memories. He wants to set us free from the power of the lies we believe. He desires his Spirit to more fully flow *within* us, doing what he most wants to do in the world *through* us, which is to bring the good news of his Kingdom to this earth through however he has gifted us. He knows who we are and who God planned for us to be. And he calls each of us "daughter."

PRAYER

Lord Jesus, thank you that amid the chaos and noise of our lives, you see us, hear us, know us and want to be with us. Thank you that you stopped and healed this woman even when you were desperately needed elsewhere. You weren't too busy for her, and you aren't too busy for us, either. We are grateful you are always open, available, and you welcome us. You already know what we need even before we know it and you gladly walk with us through our struggles.

Thank you for calling her "Daughter," and for welcoming each of us as your daughter.

Father God, thank you that you have a heart for each woman reading this book who struggles medically, who is scared about what is happening in her body. Help her to hold onto hope. Please give her your strength as she seeks answers and healing.

For the woman who has finally received a scary diagnosis, we pray for complete healing from all disease. Wherever there is a virus, bacteria, toxin, or cancer, or any other form of disease or anything disabling, please expel it all from her body. Strengthen her immune system. Renew and realign her body. Let her be like the woman in this story who touched the hem of your coat and was healed. Let your power course through her body and restore it to a state of wellness and wholeness.

For any woman who experiences irregularities and emotional swings with her hormones and monthly cycle, please give her an extra dose of your compassion and tenderness all month long. And for the woman who is in the middle of the menopause process, please calm her, cool her, and help her sleep.

Finally, Lord, for any woman whose future includes complete healing on the other side of this life, please give her your strength to make it to the finish line and then lovingly and gently lead her home when it is her time to come home to you.

In Jesus Christ's name, Amen!

QUESTIONS FOR PERSONAL REFLECTION AND GROUP SHARING

1. What do you notice about the heart, mind, and character of Jesus in this story?
2. The woman in this story was desperate to be healed but was despairing it would ever happen until she met Jesus. Where do you need healing, whether physical, mental, emotional, spiritual, or social?
3. Tell about a time in your life when something happened that made you feel unclean, unwanted, or excluded by others?
4. Those twelve years left an imprint on this woman's heart and mind, and she likely believed lies that didn't match God's perspective of who she was. How did your experiences effect what lies *feel* true for you?
    A. Lies about yourself and your worth?
    B. Lies about others?
    C. Lies about God?

5. What do you think it means to be the daughter of the King? How might your life be different if you fully saw yourself that way?

AN EXERCISE TO TRY

If you still have periods, get an old-fashioned paper calendar. (You *can* track it on your phone, but it is harder to see a whole month at a time, which is important to be able to do). At the end of the day, write 2 or 3 adjectives on the calendar that describe, overall, how you felt that day, for example, "irritable and snarly," "anxious and stressed," "sad and insecure," or "peaceful and calm." Write down whatever words come to your mind. Look at the whole of your day, not just if you had one negative experience. Then every day during your period, mark an X on the calendar. Do this for at least six months and notice if there is a pattern to the ups and downs in your moods. It's easier to give yourself grace when you know that your mood is connected to something biological and hormonal rather than something being "wrong" with you. This can help to eliminate, or at least modify, the self-criticism so many women engage in. Even if you are postmenopausal, your hormones still affect you, though at lower levels, so this exercise can even be helpful for you too (minus the X's, of course).

THREE

A Scandalous Woman

LUKE 7:36-50

Have you ever felt like you were carrying a burden that was much too heavy? Maybe you've felt the loss of something important to you: a job, a significant relationship, finances, or even your home? Perhaps you made it through a natural disaster and escaped injury but then the long clean-up and rebuild began. Or maybe you experienced a trauma and now lots of things remind you of it, which trigger feelings of shame, anxiety, hurt, or anger.

"When is it going to end?" you might wonder.

Finally, time passed, help arrived, the burden was lifted, things worked out, order was restored, and healing occurred. What a relief when it was over and you could finally relax and take a deep breath. What gratitude did you feel and how did you express it?

In Luke 7:36-50, we read about a woman who carried a heavy burden that Jesus lifted and removed. She expressed her gratitude in a very unorthodox way. With little care about what others thought, she broke every rule of etiquette to say, "Thank you." Her actions were considered scandalous by those who observed them. It earned her judgement and scorn from the religious leaders but acceptance, compassion, and grace from Jesus.

THE STORY

"Come to my house for dinner," Simon said to Jesus.

This story begins with an invitation from a member of the Pharisees, a group of religious leaders of the Sanhedrin, the highest Jewish court. Jesus was an itinerant teacher who preached, "The time has come. The Kingdom of God is near. Repent and believe the Good News," as he traveled from village to village. (Mark 1:15)

What expectations would you have if you received a dinner invitation?

Where I grew up in Northern Kentucky, my family always greeted guests with an enthusiastic, "Come in! It's so nice to see you," as they opened the door. After a handshake or a hug, you would be told, "Have a seat. Make yourself at home." You'd be invited to a table filled with delicious food and told, "Fill up your plate, don't be shy." "Would you like a second helping?" "Can I refill your glass?" "How about dessert?"

Greeted in this way, you'd feel welcome, right? Showing hospitality was highly valued in Jesus' day also. It was considered an honor to be both a guest and a host.

Perhaps earlier that day Jesus had visited the synagogue where he was invited to read from the Torah and teach on what he'd read. No doubt his reputation as a teacher and healer preceded him. Simon's curiosity about Jesus was likely piqued.

Was Simon really interested in the teachings of this new rabbi? Did he hope to learn from him? Many in the crowds who followed Jesus said he spoke as one with genuine authority unlike some of their Jewish leaders. Perhaps that stirred Simon's interest.

Or was Simon more interested in protecting his own religious traditions? Maybe he thought:

"I'll have Jesus come for dinner. I'll see for myself if he is a true follower of the law or if he's someone who will lead our people astray."

Jesus taught, "God loves sinners," but that collided with what the Pharisees taught. They believed God only loved the righteous, or those who strived to keep the 613 Jewish laws that dictated every part of their lives.[1] If that was not what Jesus taught it would be concerning to Simon. Maybe Simon needed to make sure this young upstart rabbi wouldn't undermine their traditions. As a leader, Simon no doubt believed he had an obligation to uphold the Law and the hierarchy of power in the Jewish nation and to protect people from false prophets.

Based on Simon's actions as he welcomed Jesus that day, we can assume Simon was *not* interested in what Jesus could teach him. Rather, he likely just wanted to judge for himself if Jesus was one of them or not.

Back then if someone extended hospitality, in addition to food, drink, and a place to rest, upon arrival the guest would receive a kiss of welcome on the cheek. Someone (often a servant) would wash the road's dust from the traveler's feet and would provide olive oil to clean their hands. The guest would then be invited to lounge on one of the couches around the table with the guest of honor being given the best seat. Traditionally, no prayer of blessing was offered until all guests had been accorded this kind of hospitality.[2]

But that *isn't* what happened that day.

None of those things were offered to Jesus. It's likely everyone who saw it would have understood the significance of it: Jesus was not a genuinely welcomed guest. To not offer these common courtesies was considered an insult. It was understandable for a guest to leave if they had not been welcomed in the customary manner. It was the equivalent of saying, "You're not *really* welcome here."[3] Jesus didn't take offense and leave, though. Instead, he used what happened to provide a lesson about love and forgiveness to those in the room.

Who was the woman in Luke 7 who broke the etiquette rules? She was not an invited guest nor a servant in Simon's household. Because she was not part of the social and religious elite, her presence that day would have been unusual. But it was her actions that were highly scandalous.

It's logical to assume a previous encounter with Jesus resulted in such feelings of gratitude she wanted to do something tangible to express thanks. Perhaps she'd heard Jesus was invited to dinner at Simon's house. Maybe she wanted to tell him his words had healed her heart, lifted a heavy burden, and given her hope for the future. An idea came to her of how to express her gratitude to him. She took an alabaster jar of expensive perfumed oil and hastily made her way to Simon's house.

It's possible when this woman first met Jesus, she'd desperately needed to know she was worth something to someone. Maybe she believed lies like, "I'm unacceptable. I'm worthless." Perhaps it was the first time she'd heard, "You are deeply loved and accepted by God," and "Your sins can be forgiven and washed away."

The religious teachers did not teach this message of grace. They taught that only those who kept all parts of the Law were acceptable to God. Hearing Jesus speak of this new, profound idea likely flooded her heart and mind with light and joy. Out of gratitude she wanted to offer him a gift. Perhaps she initially meant her action to be something she did quietly, unobtrusively while other guests were getting seated. But that also is not what happened.

In a typical home at that time, guests gathered at a low table surrounded by couches, positioned so guests could recline with their heads closest to the table. In his book, *Jesus Through Middle Eastern Eyes*, Kenneth Bailey[4] points out that scripture says, "he entered and reclined." Bailey notes that in the Middle Eastern Jewish tradition, the eldest guest was expected to recline first and then others after that according to their age with the youngest seated last. Since Jesus was only about 30 years old probably many of the men in the room were older than he was. But, Bailey points out, when Jesus entered the home and was not given the usual courtesies, he went ahead and reclined. That may have been the first moment when those who observed it quietly thought, "Umm, *awkward*," since Jesus wasn't the oldest man present. That also meant Jesus' head and hands were in a position the woman could not easily reach.

I wonder if, as she watched for her chance to offer her gift, she observed, as did everyone present, what lack of hospitality was shown to Jesus. I imagine her becoming indignant: this man who healed so many people was being insulted! She might have felt appalled and saddened for him. Those actions went against their cultural norms of hospitality. It brought tears to her eyes to see him treated that way.

Finally, it seems to me, she could no longer stand it. She suddenly knew her original reason for going to Simon's house to express gratitude to Jesus needed to expand. Though she may have felt uncomfortable and knew she would be judged negatively by everyone, she still followed her heart. *She* would welcome him. *She* would take on the role of servant and would extend the hospitality he should have received. Though she could not easily reach his hands and head she was able to reach his feet. She used what water was available, her tears. She had no towel to dry his feet, so she used her hair. She kissed them and anointed them with the perfumed oil from the jar.

Everyone in that room except Jesus was shocked, even horrified! Everything suddenly got quiet as they all turned to stare at this spectacle.

Simon's first thoughts were of judgement. "If this man were a prophet, he would know who was touching him and what kind of woman she is, that she is a sinner." (Luke 7:39)

"A sinner." That's the word used to describe her in the King James Version and in the New Revised Standard Version translations of the Bible. In verse 37, the New International Version describes her as a woman who had lived a sinful life. The New

English version called her "a woman living an immoral life in the town." The First Nations Version paraphrased it that she was "an outcast with broken ways."

We don't know what she did to earn that reputation. In that culture for a woman to let down her hair and allow it to be seen in public was considered sinful and was something only a prostitute would do. A man's honor would have been greatly diminished if his wife had uncovered and loosened her hair in public. In his book, *Jesus Through Middle Eastern Eyes,* Kenneth Bailey goes on to say that would've been seen as legitimate grounds for divorce.[5]

Regardless of her prior reputation, her actions proved to Simon and others that she was shameful, sinful, and immoral. The idea Jesus would allow any woman to touch him in public, much less a woman this scandalous would've taken away any credibility he might have had with most of those present. Probably Simon and his cohorts thought Jesus should have recoiled from this woman and severely rebuked her.

Of course, that is not what Jesus did.

Jesus knew what Simon and everyone in the room were thinking. He knew they all judged him and the woman negatively. One thing about Jesus though, he never missed an opportunity to teach the truth.

In the uneasy quietness of that moment Jesus spoke up and said, "Simon, I have something to tell you." (vs. 40)

"Tell me, teacher," Simon answered.

So, Jesus told the parable of a moneylender who had loaned money to two people, to one five hundred Denarii (500 pieces of silver) and to the other 50 Denarii (50 pieces of silver). One Denarii was what the wage would've been for a day's work as a common laborer, so the men would have had to work 500 days and 50 days, respectively, to pay their debts. Jesus said when it came payback time neither could repay it.[6]

Everyone listening knew the consequences of not paying back a loan to a moneylender. The person with the debt could be sent to jail until all the money was repaid by family and friends. Or the debtor might be required to become a slave to the lender.

Surprisingly, Jesus described a different outcome. "This moneylender cancelled the debt both men owed." And then Jesus asked Simon the big question,

"Which man would love him more?" (vs. 42)

Simon hesitantly replied, "I suppose the one who had the bigger debt cancelled." (vs. 43)

Jesus affirmed Simon's answer and then said something surprising. Jesus compared Simon to the woman. Simon saw himself as righteous and believed he had little for which he needed forgiveness because he followed all the rules. He and most everyone there likely believed the woman had sinned so much and broken so many rules her sins were unforgivable.

But Jesus turned everything around. He compared the hospitality Simon neglected to extend to what the woman offered him. Each one's action showed who they really were. The woman was humble and repentant but also bold and courageous enough to break the man-made rules about social propriety. Simon was arrogant and judgmental of anyone he thought was a rule-breaker.

Jesus pointed out, "Her many sins have been forgiven for she loved much. But he who has been forgiven little loves little." (Luke 7:47)

Jesus then turned to the woman and said these profound words, "Your sins are forgiven. Your faith has saved you. Go in peace." (Luke 7:50)

Those in the room were aghast! Imagine the conversations that may have occurred among the guests. "What? So, he thinks he can forgive sin? Who does he think he is...God?"

Imagine the shock and indignation that Jesus had the audacity to believe he could forgive sins. Maybe this was where the leaders first began to fixate on how to get rid of him.

So, what burden did this woman carry? We're not given

much information so we can only guess. Perhaps she was rejected because she didn't fit the cultural norms of what a woman was expected to be and do. Maybe she'd experienced trauma in her childhood and had spent her adult life living with the negative effects. Perhaps she had done things or made decisions that negatively impacted others' lives, which she now regretted. Poverty was common and if she was a widow, maybe it was difficult to feed and clothe her family. Perhaps she had turned to prostitution and had used her body in ways that felt shameful to her just to feed her children.

Jesus released her from the heavy burden she'd carried. He helped her reconnect with her truest self, the person God designed her to be before she ever sinned and was sinned against. Maybe for the first time she tuned in to what her soul really needed and wanted.

It's possible her intention in bringing the jar of perfume to Jesus was to symbolically say, "I repent. I will not engage in this again. I give this to you to prove I am done with this chapter of my life. Since you have forgiven me, I am a new woman. I no longer need this. I lay it at your feet. Thank you, thank you, thank you!"

A footnote in the NIV Study Bible about Luke 7:47 says, "Only those who realize the depths of their sin can appreciate the full forgiveness that God offers them."[7] Yes, this woman was healed and transformed because, first, she realized the depths of her sin and her own woundedness. She admitted to herself and to Jesus that her life was not in alignment with God's plan for her and she wanted to change. Second, she experienced healing and transformation as she opened her heart and mind to receive the mercy, love, and grace Jesus so extravagantly offered to her.

Jesus knew the pain in her life that likely contributed to her sin. He knew where, when, why, and how that sin began to take root within her. He knew what lies she believed about herself, others, and God. He understood the personal choices she had made as well as what societal factors had worked against her.

He also knew the original design and plan God had for her life and how she had missed the mark on that. And yet, he loved her, forgave her, cleaned out any residue of all that pain and sin. And then he restored her identity back to the original version God had of her when he designed her.

WHAT CAN WE LEARN FROM THIS STORY?

This woman was a rule-breaker, but she was still accepted and loved by Jesus. In fact, Jesus loves both rule-breakers and rule-keepers but being a rule-keeper is not what wins his affirmation and being a rule-breaker doesn't insure condemnation.

If you tend to be a rule-keeper, ask yourself: "What messages did I receive as a child about the consequences of breaking a rule? What fearful thing do I want to avoid? Or, what positives do I hope to receive?" Maybe when you were growing up, you learned that breaking a rule meant Mom or Dad or some other authority figure would withhold affection or dole out severe punishment. Maybe you learned it was safer to be a rule-keeper. Did you gain affirmation for being a rule-keeper? Last, ask yourself, "Are there *lies* I believe that contribute to me being a rule-keeper, and what truth does Jesus want me to know about that?"

On the other hand, if you tend to be a rule-breaker, some questions to ask yourself are: "What prompted me to become a rule-breaker?" "Did someone try to control me and make me conform? Or "Did I gain positive affirmation from someone when I broke the rules?" Maybe your junior high peers cheered you on when you broke the rules. Last, "What *lies* might I believe that contribute to me being a rule-breaker, and what truth does Jesus want me to know about that?"

Both rule-breakers and rule-keepers can be important to

God. Looking back in history we can find rules in place that discriminated against and harmed some people, usually the most vulnerable. God used courageous, bold rule-breakers to help change those rules. We also find instances when some people were trying to take away rules that protected the most vulnerable. God used strong, caring rule-keepers to prevent that from happening.

What Jesus most looks at is our motives. He notices what is done in love. Does breaking or keeping a rule harm or help someone? This woman broke societal rules because of her love for him. Jesus responded to her with compassion and grace because he knew she acted out of love.

Whether your tendency is to be a rule-keeper or a rule-breaker, what might happen if you invite Jesus to use that quality in whatever way he desires?

This woman had a big, bold personality that was likely influenced by her inborn temperament. Though the religious leaders saw her as disgusting, Jesus recognized her truest self and fully loved and accepted her. You also are totally loved and accepted by Jesus regardless of your personality, inborn temperament, or how others see you.

She did something bold and risky. I wonder how much her temperament influenced her actions. Is it possible this contributed to her lack of acceptance by others?

Sometimes extraverted, bold, strong women who have a big personality get misunderstood today. If that is you, Jesus understands you might have been told, "You're too much, too emotional. You need to quiet down, be less, speak less, stop being so passionate." Just like Jesus was not embarrassed by this woman's actions, he is also not put off by those qualities in you. You were designed by God with a particular personality and temperament for a reason.

Sometimes, though, women who are quieter, more introverted, and reticent to speak out get overlooked. Jesus knows the ways you might not have been seen or heard because of that. You also were designed by God with a particular temperament for a reason.

Science indicates we are born with our temperament already in place. A thirty-year study (New York Longitudinal Study) by child psychiatrists, Dr. Stella Chess and Dr. Alexander Thomas challenged a common belief at that time, "Babies are born as a blank slate." Their hypothesis was that, instead, we were born with a particular temperament. They studied 138 babies on nine behavioral characteristics and retested them multiple times from infancy through young adulthood. Each time they were evaluated on the same characteristics, they scored the same as they had when they were babies.[8] This study has been replicated many times since then and it now is normally accepted that we were each born with our temperament already in place.

Temperament also is one indicator of our life's purpose. We were designed by God for a reason, and part of that design includes our inborn temperament. Jesus wants us to be who he planned for us to be so we can do in our lives what he planned for us to do. So, if the world judges you for being too loud or too quiet, know that you were designed by God in this way for a reason and you are still accepted and valued by him.

What do you know about your inborn temperament and how that influences your life?

This woman seems to have allowed Jesus entrance into all the rooms of her heart and mind, even those where pain and brokenness are located. Jesus wants you to invite him into whatever pain, shame, and brokenness you carry, also.

We don't know what pain this woman invited Jesus to come into. She hid nothing from him but welcomed him and allowed him to see every part of her life. Jesus wants a similar invitation from you.

Perhaps an analogy will help us understand this idea a little better: In 1 Corinthians 6:19 we read that our body is the temple of the Holy Spirit. He lives within us when we invite him into our life. That means he takes up residence within us. His home is our heart and mind. Since most homes have more than one room, it's helpful to think of our heart and mind having various "rooms" into which we can invite Jesus.

Thinking of that reminds me of my friend Kathy's two-story colonial style home. It offers an illustration about being invited into various rooms. When I visit Kathy, I come in through the front door, into a foyer. It's the place where she greets me and I can hang up my coat.

To the left and right of the foyer are a formal living room and a dining room. Kathy mostly uses those rooms for special occasions like holiday dinners or a wedding or baby shower. They are beautifully decorated. Her best dishes and linens are used there. But as attractive as the rooms are, it's harder to relax and be myself in them. I'm more conscious of manners and am extra careful not to spill something or accidentally knock something over. I certainly would never put my feet up on the coffee table.

When I visit Kathy, because we are dear friends, she invites me to go past those rooms to an informal family room and kitchen. Those spaces are where real life happens. It's easy to feel relaxed, comfortable, and freer to be myself there. It's the kind of place where I *can* put my feet on the coffee table. Those rooms are places where people get to know each other at a deeper level, spaces where families and friends spend quality time and share their hearts with one another.

Kathy's house gives us a picture of what a relationship with Jesus could look like if we invite him into all the rooms of our heart and mind. A question to ask yourself would be, "How far into my heart and mind have I invited Jesus?"

Is your relationship with Jesus one that stays in the foyer of your heart and mind? Is he little more than an acquaintance? Is your faith something you easily put off and on, like a coat hanging on a coat rack beside the door?

Or have you mostly invited Jesus into the formal rooms of your heart and mind but no further in? If so, it might seem to you that being a Christian is about being a rule keeper. If obeying all the rules is a high priority in how you live your life, it's possible you might have a better understanding of God's might, power, and judgement than His mercy, love, and grace. It's possible to have a lot of knowledge about Jesus and the Bible but still have an emotional disconnect between you and him. It might be easier to be generous with your gifts, strengths, and talents but more difficult to admit your weaknesses, limitations, and sins to others. If you've only invited Jesus into the "formal rooms" of your heart and mind, you might be missing out on the peace that comes with being your authentic self with Jesus and other believers.

If you have invited Jesus into the family room of their heart and mind you probably experience regular intimacy with Jesus. Maybe you see him as your best friend. You probably know you can share anything with him—whatever is messy in your life, whatever weaknesses you have—and trust you will still be accepted and loved. You probably also have deeper intimacy with other believers. You seek to be authentic and more readily admit to the struggles, sin, or messes in your life as well as your strengths and gifts. Your understanding of God is probably more focused on his love, mercy, and grace than on his might, power, and judgment.

Unfortunately, life is not always family room quality. Sometimes it's difficult. In fact, sometimes life *stinks*, which reminds me of the little house where I was raised.

I grew up in the country on five acres of land, surrounded by trees and fields. Our house was in a valley between a long, slowly sloping hill behind the house and a short, steep hill covered with woods in front of the house. At the bottom of that valley was a road that followed a little creek. Our house was about two hundred feet from the creek.

Since it was country living there was no sewer system. Our home had a septic tank in the front yard about 25 to 30 feet from the front porch buried about six feet deep. A septic tank holds all the water and waste products from a flushed toilet.

As kids we never thought about that septic tank. The grass grew over the tank the same as it grew elsewhere in our yard. We played games in the yard as though it was not there. The only time we remembered it was when it rained long and hard. The water would roll down those hills, the creek would rise, and what was in that septic tank would back up into our basement. What a stinky mess!

I remember my dad putting on rubber boots and gloves to clean up the mess. He had a 50-foot metal rope-like tool he called a "snake," and he would use that to "snake out" whatever had gotten stuck in the pipe. He would put that snake in the floor drain and start pushing. Once he got things unstuck the mess would drain back into the septic tank. Then Dad would scrub the floor with soap and bleach. Thankfully, Dad finally solved the problem but until it was fixed, we could expect a smelly mess whenever there was an overabundance of rain.

Now you probably know where I am going with this story, don't you? So, back to our analogy about inviting Jesus into the various rooms of our heart and mind...

Jesus wants to be invited into all the rooms of your heart, not just the foyer or formal rooms. Not just the family room where he is our best friend. He also wants us to invite him into the basement of our life where the septic tank is backing up. We all have a basement, and we all have stuff that backs up in it periodically. It's his mercy that "snakes" out what is blocked in us and it's his love and grace that act as the soap and bleach that cleanses us.

How do you know if something is backing up in the basement of your heart and mind? Here are a few examples: sometimes when you feel afraid, worried, irritable, resentful, impatient, jealous, or ashamed; when you feel insecure or think you don't belong; when you need to have an honest conversation with someone but you're afraid of hurting their feelings or making them angry; when you can't say "no" when asked to do another job for which you have neither time or energy.

What kinds of things could back up into the basement of someone's heart and mind? Here are examples:

1. Grief about a loss in your life you've never dealt with.
2. A sense of shame about something you did or something that was done to you.
3. A sense of longing for something you legitimately needed but didn't receive, such as acceptance or love.
4. A secret sin that you struggle with, but it holds on like a deeply rooted weed.
5. Any place where you believe lies that don't match up with Jesus' perspective of you.

Into what rooms in your heart and mind have you invited Jesus? What sometimes backs up in the basement of your heart and mind?

PRAYER

Lord, you know each woman who carries a heavy burden that weighs her down and exhausts her. She is tired, sees no end in sight, and her hope is waning. Please show her you are with her in the middle of that heaviness. Exchange your strength for her weakness.

You know the times in a woman's life where she made mistakes, did wrong, hurt someone, or hurt herself. You know when something is backing up in the "basement" of her life. You also know the ways she may have condemned herself for that. Please allow her a "realization of the depths of her sin so she can appreciate the full forgiveness that you offer her."[9] Gently bring her back to You and your plans for her life. Exchange your compassion for her self-condemnation.

Jesus, you see the woman who feels hurt from being judged. Please comfort her. Set her free from the lies she believes about herself, or the lies she fears are true.

You designed each of us in a unique and wonderful way but sometimes a woman compares herself to others and believes she is not enough – not smart, talented, attractive, lovable, or good enough. Please hold your mirror up to her and remind her of the amazing person you designed her to be.

You know each woman who has been repeatedly told, "You are too much, too loud, too passionate, too strong, and too bossy." Reassure her you designed her that way for a reason. Show her how to use those qualities in ways that bring honor to you and help build your Kingdom. Set her free of any lies she came to believe about herself because of that. Empower her to live as big, bold, loud, and strong as you need her to be so she can do whatever you are calling her to do.

You also know the woman who is self-conscious, timid, and worries about what everyone thinks of her. Bring your love, light, and truth into any memories that contribute to that and point out lies she believes about herself. Remind her of how deeply you love her and love being with her. Show her who she really is in your eyes and then empower her to enjoy being herself.

Thank you, Jesus, for the woman willing to be a spectacle for you, the woman who steps up and does something others are too anxious or embarrassed to do. When her heart beats fast because she is scared to follow your promptings, give her the same courage and boldness you gave the woman in this story.

QUESTIONS FOR PERSONAL REFLECTION AND GROUP SHARING

1. What do you notice about the heart, mind, and character of Jesus in this story?
2. If you have ever been in a place where you weren't welcomed, or you were judged negatively, how did that affect you?
3. Looking back, did you tend to be more of a rule keeper or a rule breaker? How might Jesus use that tendency for good if you "laid it down" at his feet?
4. Into what rooms of your heart and mind have you invited Jesus?
5. What sometimes "backs up in the basement" of your heart and mind? What does Jesus want to do with that?

AN EXERCISE TO TRY

If there was a time when you felt judged or unwelcomed, what happened, how old were you, and how did it affect you? Write a letter expressing compassion to any part of you who has experienced that. Write as though you are writing to your best friend.

Or, if you are currently going through a time when your heart feels heavy, sad, worried, or afraid, write a letter of encouragement to yourself as though you are talking to your best friend. Ask the Holy Spirit to give you words that align with God's truest perspective of you.

FOUR

A Despised Woman

JOHN 4:1 - 42

WHAT PICTURE COMES to your mind when you think of a well? I remember the well on my grandparents' farm in Eastern Kentucky. My family spent most vacations there. I have many sweet childhood memories: slowly waking up to the sounds of roosters crowing and cows mooing, playing in the cool, green shade of the woods around the house, wading in the sparkling water of a little stream down in the bottom land of the 100-plus acre farm, smelling the earthy scent of a freshly plowed garden and newly mowed hay, hearing the beautiful symphony of birds flying in and out of the trees.

There was one memory, though, that left an indelible imprint on my mind: the house had no running water. As a kid it seemed like both a curse and a blessing. It was like a curse because that meant we had to use the outhouse and even worse, we had to be on the lookout for snakes! It was a blessing because water drawn from the well was the coldest, sweetest, most refreshing water I ever drank.

In John 4 we read about a well that was famous in Jesus' day. Actually, this story is about three wells. The first well was like my grandparents' well. It was a real well that provided water for the people and flocks who lived nearby. It was called Jacob's

Well and had been in the land of Samaria for hundreds of years. Amazingly, it's still in existence today, located in the area known as the West Bank, though it's now located inside a Greek Orthodox church. The second well in our story is a metaphorical one that represents the deep pain and soul-thirstiness a woman in the story experienced and the ways she tried to assuage her thirst. The third well represents the life-giving spiritual water Jesus offered to the woman.

THE STORY

One day Jesus and his disciples were traveling through the land of Samaria, and they stopped at Jacob's Well. The disciples went into town to buy food while Jesus rested near the well. Just then a Samaritan woman came to the well seeking water. It was one of those necessary, daily tasks she had to do to have water for drinking, cooking, and cleaning. What was unusual about this woman is she was alone. It was also the hottest time of the day. It was customary for women to go to the well together because it was safer, more respectable, and offered some community to the women of Sychar, the nearby town. They usually went early in the morning and in the evening when it was cooler.

Why was this woman alone? Scripture doesn't give us her backstory so we can only make assumptions. Is it possible she was avoiding someone? Had she previously gone to the well hoping to connect with other women but had been ignored? Were hurtful words previously spoken to her? Has she been judged negatively? Did she believe lies that she was unwanted, rejected, invisible? If so, how and when did it start and how long had it continued before she decided to no longer put herself in the position of facing hurt and shame every day?

The culture in Jesus' day placed greater value on a sense of "we" versus "me" than what we value in our culture today. Of course, it can be incredibly painful and lonely for any woman to be rejected by a group and have no place of belonging. A woman who was shunned and cut off from community would have experienced immense shame.

Or possibly a different scenario played out. Maybe she originally thought she was better than them. When she was younger, perhaps she was the girl all the boys of Sychar hoped to marry someday. Maybe she had proudly looked down on the other young women, believing the lie that they didn't measure up to her. Maybe she pridefully acted in a snobbish manner so they all rejected her. After many years, perhaps this pattern was so well established she no longer looked to women for friendships.

Regardless of the reason she was alone, either scenario leads us to the second kind of well. This Samaritan woman had been drinking from a well of pain and emptiness for many years. Perhaps that came from a thirstiness within her soul to find a place of belonging and love but the water in that well had turned bitter or polluted or had completely run dry. That day when she trudged out to Jacob's Well, she was emotionally and spiritually dying of thirst because there was no longer any good water in any well from which she drank: no family, friends, tribe, network of support, and no love. And that may be how she found herself all alone in the middle of a hot and dusty day with the sun beating down on her as she did some mindless, thankless chore.

That day, however, she found someone who offered her water from a third kind of well, one vastly different from the other two wells. It was a well that would never run dry, one that would always provide spiritual thirst-quenching water to anyone seeking it. She came to Jacob's Well for water from the first kind of well. She had been drinking from the second kind of well for many years. But down deep, what she longed for was water from the third kind of well. Her deepest desire was to find a well that would offer a steady stream of life-giving, soul-renewing spiritual water instead of an empty or bitter bucket of promises. A well that would never run dry.

She approached the well where a man was alone. Not the

safest or wisest thing to do. She apparently ignored her self-preservation instinct and continued towards her goal of completing the task. How fortunate she was, though, because that man resting beside the well was Jesus.

"Will you give me a drink?" (John 4:7)

Imagine her shock that a Jewish man who was not supposed to interact with a woman in public, much less a Samaritan woman, would ask her for a drink of water! She was confused when he told her if she knew who she was talking to she would ask him for a drink.

"Uh, excuse me, but you have neither a bucket nor a cup, and the well is deep," she said. "And... *exactly* how do you think you could give me a drink of water?" may have gone through her mind.

"Are you greater than our ancestor Jacob, who gave us the well?" she asked. (John 4:12) "So..., you think you can perform some kind of miracle here?" she may have thought.

"Everyone who drinks this water will be thirsty again but whoever drinks the water I give them will never be thirsty. The water I give them will become in them a spring of water gushing up to eternal life." Jesus told her. (John 4:13)

Well, now, that got her attention. If he could give her water that would allow her to never have to go out to that well ever again, how great that would be! Maybe she would never have to face that group of women again nor the shame of being rejected. Maybe she would never have to feel stigmatized by her past or feel the sting of being alone and lonely ever again. Maybe all of that would go away.

"Sir, give me this water, so that I may never be thirsty or have to keep coming here to draw water," she said. "Absolutely, yes!" she may have excitedly thought.

And maybe she was hoping Jesus would just say, "Alrighty then, one order of my kind of water coming right up."

Of course, that is not what he said.

His next statement probably surprised her even more. "Go call your husband and then come back," Jesus told her.

Wait...what?

"I have no husband," she said. And *here* is where it gets more interesting.

"You're right. You've had five husbands and the man you are with now is not your husband," Jesus told her.

This scripture has often been interpreted that she was a very loose, immoral woman. There is likely more to the story, though. Yes, she had been married five times, something many Christians today would judge as scandalous. But what did it mean back then? It either meant she was a widow five times, or she was divorced by five husbands, or some combination of the two.

First, let's talk about divorce back then. There were two schools of thought taught by influential rabbis, Shammai and Hillel. According to the Shammai teachings, a man could divorce his wife only in the case of infidelity. But the Hillel school of thought held that a man could divorce his wife for such simple reasons as if she did not cook his meals the way he wanted.[1] And according to Hillel, a man was obligated to divorce his wife if she was infertile and did not produce a child after ten years of marriage.[2] Perhaps this Samaritan woman struggled with infertility. Maybe she was unable to get pregnant. Could this be why she'd had five husbands?

In that culture, infertility was considered a consequence of her sin. It would have held much stigma and shame. So, perhaps this was the real reason this woman avoided the other women at the well. To hang out with other women who talked about babies and motherhood when she couldn't be part of those conversations may have felt incredibly sad and humiliating for her.

In that culture a woman had no rights to oppose a divorce, nor did she have the right to divorce her husband, so we know divorce was not something she initiated. What options were available to a woman whose husband divorced her? First, the dowry her father had given to her future husband or husband's father upon their marriage was supposed to be returned to her. Sometimes that happened but sometimes it did not. If she received it, she could live on that for a while. Second, she could return to her family of origin and live with her father if he was still alive or with other relatives if they would take her in. Third, she could seek to marry someone else, though that wasn't easy in that culture. If none of those options were available, she would be in a precarious position. The only options available might be to resort to begging for money for food or to turn to prostitution.[3]

A second possibility for this woman is if she had been widowed five times. In that culture, a man was obligated to marry his older brother's widow. Maybe each man she married had been a brother of the husband who had just died. In most situations, a woman could not inherit money from her husband if he died, as it was passed down to his sons. She could, however, come under their care. If the sons were young, she could take care of the property until the sons were old enough to inherit it. But if she had no sons, if her deceased husband had no brother, if her father was no longer alive, and if her family could not take her in, again, she likely would have no means of support. The choices available to her would again be limited.

Based on what Jesus said, we know she was in a relationship with a man to whom she was not married. Perhaps she was in an adulterous relationship or living with a man who didn't care enough about her to marry her. But there is one other possibility. Perhaps after the ending of her most recent marriage whether by divorce or the death of her spouse she might have sold herself as a concubine to a man to avoid being homeless and a beggar.[4] Being a concubine was a step above being a slave. However, that likely would have been a choice open more to a woman who had the capacity to produce a baby.

We often want to simply label this woman as sinful without

looking at the context of her life and the desperation she may have faced. Jesus refused to do that, though. He knew exactly what had happened in her life and all the grief she'd experienced. He understood fully the well of pain she drank from for many years, and he willingly offered her compassion and truth spoken in a non-condemnatory way.

So, what do people do when something they want to remain hidden is exposed? Some get defensive and do what she did next. She tried to deflect attention away from the truth Jesus pointed out about her and to steer the conversation back to safer, more neutral grounds.

"I see you are a prophet. Our ancestors worshiped on this mountain but you Jews think Jerusalem is where people should worship." (John 4:19)

Jesus saw through her attempt to redirect the conversation, and he told her something profound. He told her the day was coming when people would neither worship on that mountain nor in Jerusalem. He told her true worshippers would worship in spirit and truth, and God was seeking that kind of worshipper.

Her answer to him may have indicated she was now listening with her heart and not just her head when she said, "I know that Messiah is coming. When he comes, he will explain everything to us." (John 4:25)

Did Jesus detect a longing within her for that? Did he notice a desire for true worship and a relationship with the Almighty? Perhaps he did because he chose to reveal to *her*, a Samaritan woman, a woman hated by the Jews and maybe by her own people, and someone he was not even supposed to talk to, that indeed, he was the Messiah. He hadn't revealed that to anyone yet. Yes, *he* was the one for whom her people were waiting. *He* was the one for whom the Jews were waiting. And *he* was the one she was waiting for whether she consciously knew it or not.

How his words and response to her must have touched her

heart! How long had it been since someone had treated her with respect, had listened to what she had to say, and had spoken truth into her life with no condemnation? In fact, had anyone ever cared enough about her to step outside of society's rules and regulations regarding public interactions between a man and a woman and to treat her as a real person instead of a piece of property?

Not likely.

That might be why hope suddenly burst into her heart, and she couldn't contain it. She wanted to share with others in her town what she had experienced. Leaving her water jar behind she ran back to town and exclaimed to anyone she met, "Come, see a man who told me everything I ever did. Could this be the Christ?" (vs. 29). Her enthusiasm caught people's attention, and the people of the town began to stream out to the well where Jesus was.

At first, they listened to Jesus because of her enthusiastic invitation. Soon they believed for themselves that, indeed, Jesus was the true Messiah for whom they had been waiting. They asked him to stay for a while and teach them, so he took two days out of his journey to Galilee to spend time with them in Samaria. He introduced them to the truth that God welcomes every person into His kingdom who welcomes Jesus into their lives. Even those who have been rejected and shunned by others. Even those who had made messes of their lives and whose lives were far from perfect. Even those whose bodies were infertile. Yes, even those who repeatedly drank from the same well of pain and brokenness, desperately trying to get filled up with something they legitimately needed but could never find in their polluted or dry wells.

That day this woman of Samaria found the answer to the thirst in her soul she had experienced for many years. That day she discovered what Jesus meant when he said, "The water I give will become a spring of water gushing up to eternal life."

And that day she took her first drink of the coldest, sweetest, most refreshing spiritual water she ever tasted.

WHAT CAN WE LEARN FROM THIS STORY?

Jesus wanted a relationship with this woman even though, as a Samaritan, she was scorned and hated by the Jews of that day. Jesus also wants a relationship with us whether we are part of the "in-crowd" or not, regardless of who has been against us.

The New Testament is full of stories of people with whom Jesus spent time. Often, they were the common folks, those who did the menial jobs the social elite would never do. He spent time with those who couldn't afford to meticulously keep all 613 commandments listed in the Torah (the first five books of the Bible). Jesus wasn't afraid to hang out with those who were seen by the religious leaders as "riffraff," the ones who did the dirty, sweaty jobs. Though Jesus wasn't opposed to hanging out with the wealthy and the religious, he spent most of his time with those who were looked down on by the religious leaders.

He also loves to spend time with each of us, regardless of where we are on the social ladder, high or low. He doesn't use the same lenses—social status, wealth, level of education, business success, health, skills, talents, religion, politics, color of skin, gender, or cultural expectations—to determine who he'll spend time with. He wants to spend time with each of us even if we:

- Were the "lowest of the low" in junior high school, the one everyone bullied.
- Never belonged to the popular crowd.
- Failed at school, or in a job, or in a marriage, or as a parent.

- Think we don't know enough, don't have enough, or aren't enough.
- Believe lies about our worth that got tattooed on our heart and mind from past painful experiences.

What interferes with you hanging out with Jesus? What interferes with you believing Jesus wants to hang out with you?

Jesus knew the ways this woman had been hurt. He also fully knows and cares deeply about the ways we have each been hurt in life.

If you watch the news or scroll through social media, you know there are many people in pain. It's been my privilege as a therapist to hear the stories of some. Sometimes people seem confident on the outside but behind their facade, many struggle internally with insecurity, anxiety, shame, and hurt. Some talk of feeling like an imposter and fear others will discover they are a fraud. Others describe painful scenes from their younger years that continue to flash in their mind. Many of them believe some variation of the five kinds of lies: *Possibility, Responsibility, Capability, Acceptability, or Vulnerability Lies.*

How do I know Jesus cares deeply about us? First, Scripture tells us he does. "He heals the brokenhearted and binds up their wounds." (Psalm 147:3, NRSV) This is one of many passages that talk about his love. Second, despite all the pain reported in the news, there is still evidence of love and kindness in the world. There are people who seek to care as Jesus cared, to be his hands and feet, eyes and ears, heart, mind, and voice in our world today. They choose to be available for God to express his love through them to those who are hurting.

Third, I care a lot about people—my family, friends, and those with whom I work. If I, an imperfect human, can care that much, then the One who designed me with that capacity cares way, way more than I do about what people are going through. Even when Jesus' response is not obvious and we can't see what he is doing, his compassion and care are still operative all the time and are freely offered to us.

> *What are ways you have been hurt by life?*
> *What are ways you seek to allow God's love to be expressed through you?*

Jesus already knows the things we thirst for, the lies that feel true to us, and the wells we've drunk from to try to quench our soul's thirst.

Pastor and author John Ortberg observes: "Sin is often the attempt to meet a legitimate need in an illegitimate way."[5] As a Christian therapist, that makes sense to me. When we don't get legitimate needs met in healthy ways, we often experience pain, shame, sadness, anxiety, or anger. Sometimes we turn to illegitimate ways to fill those needs.

For example, we may try to accumulate more money or things to fill a sense of emptiness inside. Or maybe to feel we have value, we do whatever we think we need to do to "climb the social or professional ladder," regardless of who it harms. Maybe in our insecurity we pretend we are strong by bullying or demeaning someone else. Or perhaps we try to rescue, fix, or control others. Maybe we try to numb or ignore our pain through such means as workaholism or an overuse of alcohol or other substances, compulsive shopping, or even "church-a-holism." We keep trying to drink from those wells because we don't know what else to do.

Jesus knows the polluted or dried up wells we drink from that keep us trapped in cycles of performance and perfectionism, rescuing and fixing, hiding and avoiding, or comparison and self-condemnation. He understands the pain we've experienced that we shouldn't have had to endure, like someone's abuse or bullying. He knows about the wells we've drunk from to quell our pain or to receive something we legitimately needed but didn't receive, such as safety, comfort, or love.

A desire to be valued, loved, and to belong are legitimate human needs but sometimes people lack opportunities to experience them in a healthy way. For example, as a therapist, I often counsel women who experienced emotional, physical, and sexual abuse. Their stories are often similar. Consider the woman who grew up in a family where she was verbally, physically, and sexually abused. She also received a lot of male attention from the time she was a child because of her beauty. While her deepest desire was to be safe, loved, cherished, and to have someone commit to her, she believed the lie that her beauty was the only avenue to find love. She turned to men repeatedly who were drawn to her because of how pretty and vivacious she was. They seemed to cherish her initially but eventually cheated on her, used her, treated her poorly, or abandoned her. She attempted to get a legitimate need for love met in an illegitimate way. The "well" she drank from was either polluted or dried up.

There is nothing ungodly about wanting to be loved, valued, and significant. In fact, *when* we feel those things, we are more in alignment with God's perspective of us. Here are some things we can do to open to his truth about us:

- Release the negative emotional charge our mind and body carry from past trauma and where legitimate needs didn't get met. We can invite Jesus to shine his light into our heart and mind and take us back through important memories where lies got installed.
- Acknowledge to him the wells we have drunk from and the illegitimate ways we tried to care for those legitimate needs.
- Ask Jesus to show us how he sees us and his truth about who we really are. Ask him to plant this truth

into any memory where there was an absence of love, kindness, or safety.
- Ask him to fill our needs with his acceptance, comfort, love, and truth.
- Identify memories when we offered compassion, kindness, and encouragement to others. Then turn around and offer that same compassion to ourselves.

It takes courage to invite Jesus to shine his light into our life and expose all this. Learning to allow Him to quench our thirst for being loved, valued, significant, and belonging is not easy. It can take some time. But when we do it, it's like taking a long, deep drink from the sweetest, most refreshing water of all.

What kind of soul-thirstiness have you experienced and what wells have you drunk from as you sought to get legitimate needs met?

Jesus knew the truth of how this woman was designed and why she was here on earth. He knew we would each need to read her story someday. He also knows the full truth about the beautiful way God designed each of us. He knows our purpose and what plans he originally had for our lives.

He knows we have each been made in the image of God. We see it in the fact that no one has a fingerprint exactly like ours. Jesus longs for us to be free to embrace his truth of who we really are as valued, loved, wanted, and welcomed.

How true does the above statement feel to you?

PRAYER

Lord Jesus, you know the places inside each of us that hold hurt, sadness, grief, shame, insecurity, fear, and anger. You know exactly what situations in our lives brought about these painful feelings and thoughts. You know the wells we have drunk from in attempts to silence or hide that pain. We invite you to gently lead us back to any memory where pain and lies still exist. Please set us free from their power. But Lord, we can't go there alone, so please go with us, hold our hand, and flood our hearts and minds with your love as we walk back through any dark pathways.

Thank you for not condemning us for those times when we have drunk from any well other than you. Thank you also, that you are always willing to help us break free from those wells and begin to drink from the water that only you offer. Thank you for your patience with us in that process.

Lord, God, you know the woman who has been hurt by some arrogance or snobbishness of another woman or who has been rejected or demeaned by her peers. Please heal that pain and allow her shame and hurt to be transformed into something beautiful, something that's a source of light for others who have also experienced that.

You also know the woman who may have contributed to the pain of another woman, who may have judged, demeaned, gossiped about, or rejected someone who longed to belong. Please stir her conscience and lead her to seek forgiveness and reconciliation.

You know how bad it feels to go through either the pain of divorce or the pain of a spouse dying. You know the enormously negative impact this has on a woman's life. For any woman who has ever experienced that, please provide comfort as well as whatever she needs to be able to grieve the losses and then live her life fully.

You also understand the pain of infertility. If any woman

reading this is experiencing this, please heal her body and prepare it for childbirth. If that is not your plan, then fill her heart and empty arms with you. Give her opportunities to give love and nurture to children, other people who need it, or even to animals. Take the love she has available to give and multiply it in beautiful ways.

May each woman who reads this come to know deep down that she is incredibly worthy of your love, even if life has not worked out for her according to whatever dreams and hopes she had. Make your love known to her in a very tangible and concrete way today.

And thank you, Jesus, that *you* are the well that will never run dry, and for the sweet water of your presence that flows through us into a world that you love.

QUESTIONS FOR PERSONAL REFLECTION AND GROUP SHARING

1. What glimpses of the heart, mind, and character of Jesus do you see in this story?
2. When have you experienced being rejected by an individual or a group? What happened and how old were you? What lies about yourself, others, or God did you come to believe?
3. What "wells" have you drunk from in attempts to numb or manage the pain from that?
4. What truth do you believe God wants you to know and believe about His view of you?
5. It is often through the painful, unjust situations in our lives we develop a deeper understanding of God's presence, guidance, strength, and love. How was your faith impacted because of difficult times in your life?

6. Once we are on the other side of a painful situation, God often brings opportunities our way for us to be a source of empathy, encouragement, wisdom, and truth to others going through the same kind of difficulty. It is a way of bringing meaning out of something painful. What are ways God has used that challenging time in your life to help someone else? Or how might God lead you to bring meaning out of your pain by helping someone else in similar pain in the future?

AN EXERCISE TO TRY

Create a timeline of the various stages in your life and what happened to you in each one. Draw a line from the beginning of the timeline to the end of it right through the middle of the page. Above the line, list what significant things happened over the course of your life that were positive happenings for you. Below the line, list what significant things happened to you that were negative. Write out what you came to believe about yourself next to those events. Use as many pieces of paper as needed to go through each stage of your life. This is not a quick, easy exercise, so take your time with it even if it takes you several weeks or a month. And please be gentle and kind to yourself as you work on this.

You can also find a series of eight visual maps "for recognizing and responding to God in my story," in the *Listen to My Life* series developed by Sibyl Towner and Sharon Swing. Map number two, "My Life Story," offers a great visual map for doing a timeline and reflecting on your past. You can find the maps at www.onelifemaps.com. You can either order the complete set of eight maps, or you can order just Map #2.

FIVE

A Discarded Woman

JOHN 8:1-10

ONE WEEKEND when my son was a toddler and my daughter a baby, we made the trek down from Chicago to my parents' home in Northern Kentucky. During that visit Mom asked me to help her go through some old boxes stored for years on shelves in the basement.

Most of the things we found simply needed to be donated or thrown away. But we found one unexpected treasure. What a surprise to find an old Lionel electric train that belonged to my brother when he was a little boy. I was thrilled because we had just transitioned our son's bedroom from a baby room to a "big boy" room. I'd decorated the room with a transportation theme since he was fascinated with trucks, fire engines, and trains. I thought it would be so cute to put that train on a shelf in his room, so I asked Mom if I could have it.

Understandably, since it belonged to my brother, she said she'd first ask if he wanted it. Of course, I understood. He was the rightful owner. I was sure he would love to have that treasure from his childhood.

I didn't think about the Lionel train again until a few years later when I visited my brother and his family. I suddenly recalled it and asked him, "Have you enjoyed your childhood treasure Mom found in a box in the basement?"

That was the first time he'd heard about it. He was excited, though, to think about finding a toy he loved and played with as a child. He planned to pick it up the next time he was at our parents' house.

Later, I told Mom, "Darrell was happy to hear you found his toy train. He looks forward to picking it up soon."

Mom hesitantly replied, "Oh... I got rid of all those boxes in the basement. A man going through the neighborhood with a truck asked people if they had anything they wanted to get rid of, so I just gave all those boxes to him." She had apparently forgotten that among the trash, was a treasure.

In John 8:1-10, we read a story of a woman who was considered by the religious leaders of that day to simply be trash or junk, but Jesus saw her true worth.

THE STORY

In Jesus' day, as in ours, what was defined as trash or junk and what was defined as treasure depended on who did the defining. Many of the religious leaders seemed to treasure wealthy men who scrupulously followed all the statutes of the Law of Moses. The common people, those who labored every day as farmers, fishermen, shepherds, and shop keepers were seen as having less value because they were unable to keep the numerous Jewish laws about remaining ceremonially clean. But anyone who was poor, a slave, a Gentile, a foreigner, a female, or chronically sick or disabled, were considered to have little value. In other words, they were seen as junk, trash, dispensable, easily discarded.

Jesus had spent the night in the garden on the Mount of Olives, a place where he often went alone to pray. Early that morning, fresh from his personal time with his Heavenly Father, he went to the place he was so passionate about, the

Temple. Apparently, some religious leaders and teachers were also out early making their way to the Temple *not* energized by their personal time with God. They were invigorated by the idea of catching Jesus right where they wanted him, in a trap.

That morning as Jesus taught in the temple the leaders interrupted him by dragging in a woman. Imagine the noise and chaos they brought to the place that was supposed to be for learning about and connecting with God. They stood her in front of Jesus and the growing crowd. They recounted what they had caught her doing, engaging in adultery. It was a sin that carried a very steep penalty: death by stoning. Jesus could probably see the terror in her eyes and hear her frightened, shallow breaths.

"Teacher, this woman was caught in the very act of committing adultery. Now in the Law, Moses commanded us to stone such a woman. Now what do you say?" (John 8:4-5, NRSV)

But Jesus knew it was a trap.

He knew if he said, "Yes, the law states that was sin and she should be stoned," then those leaders would have likely reported him to the Roman authorities as someone who advocated breaking Rome's laws. The Jews were not allowed to execute anyone without Roman permission.

But if Jesus said, "No, she should not be stoned," then they would say, "You are advocating breaking the law given to us by Moses, so you are guilty of sin."

They believed whatever answer he gave would deliver Jesus into their hands. So, Jesus chose to not participate in their drama.

Instead, he bent down and began to write in the dirt with his finger. They tried to goad him into engaging with them. But he just ignored them. Finally, he looked up at them and said these profound words:

"If any one of you is without sin let him be the first to throw a stone at her." (vs. 7)

He turned away from them and continued writing in the dirt. Amazingly, the men soon began to slip away, the oldest ones first until finally there was no one left to accuse the woman. Jesus finally looked up from his writing and saw no one in front of him except the woman.

"Woman, where are they? Has no one condemned you?" (vs. 10)

The woman answered, "No one, sir."

And Jesus said, "Then neither do I condemn you. Go now and leave your life of sin." (vs. 11)

Who was this woman? Scripture doesn't spell that out so we can only speculate. Was she younger or older? Single, married, divorced, or widowed? Was she a young woman in an arranged marriage who loved someone else but had not been permitted by her father to marry him? Was she a widow with no hope of any future marriage, with children to feed but no means to support them? Had she needed to resort to prostitution to have money for food and shelter? Had she experienced sexual abuse as a child and believed the lies that she was dirty and worthless, so was open to any man expressing something that helped her feel cared for? Was she a victim of something like our modern day "Me Too" movement, a woman forced by a man to have sex with him?

We don't know. We also don't know how exactly she was "caught in the act." Had someone spied on her to catch her, perhaps waiting for the man to leave? Or was he able to escape, leaving her with all the blame? Was she awakened from her sleep by someone barging into her home and rudely pulling her from her bed? And where was the man? If she was "caught in the act," why was he not dragged off to stand in front of Jesus also? After all, the law did not specify, "Stone *her*." It said if two people were caught in adultery, "Stone *both*." Isn't it logical their words to Jesus of "caught in the act," would include both her and the man? Is it possible she was set up, used, and betrayed?

She likely knew what would happen to her and that the verdict had already been decided. She probably assumed she would be pronounced "guilty," and the Roman authorities had already given permission for her to be executed. She also knew how the story would end. She would be dragged off to someplace away from the Temple, outside the gates of the city. A battery of stones would be flung at her until either she lost enough blood she finally died, or she was hit by a stone big enough to fatally injure her. Death by stoning usually took anywhere from twenty minutes to two hours.[1]

Have you ever been hit by a rock? Even a little one hurts, a lot! Generally, small rocks were not used but those big enough to do some damage. She knew it could be a slow, agonizing death before it would finally be over.

She probably felt not only terrified but also humiliated to be publicly dragged down the road to the Temple. It should have been a place where she found forgiveness and healing. Instead, she found only judgement and condemnation. Aside from Jesus, did anyone care anything about what she experienced? It doesn't appear so. She seems to just be considered a piece of junk or trash.

She was discardable. A "nobody." Maybe she also believed those lies. Was she just a pawn for a group of powerful men to use to bolster their sense of importance and display their righteousness. To many in the temple that day, these men probably looked and sounded like they were truly righteous and godly because they were passionate about upholding the Law. Jesus knew, though, behind their facades all they really were dedicated to was preserving their own power.

Are you curious about what Jesus was writing in the dirt? In his book, *Jesus Through Middle Eastern Eyes*, Kenneth Bailey hypothesized Jesus wrote the words of "death," or "stone her," or "kill her" to show those religious leaders that indeed, he was very knowledgeable regarding the Law.[2] His words, though, "If any one of you is without sin, let him be the first to throw a stone at her," would have prompted them to recall the scripture that said, "Surely there is not a righteous man on earth who does what is right and never sins." (Ecclesiastes 7:20 NIV). Bailey says it would have been considered shameful for any man to say he was without sin. None would have willingly picked up that first stone after hearing Jesus's words.

Or, as has been conjectured, was Jesus writing in the dirt the secret sins of each of those religious leaders? No one knows what Jesus wrote. But just imagine seeing your name and secret sin written publicly for all to see. If that is what Jesus was writing, no wonder the men began to disappear.

It seems this woman was used and abused emotionally, sexually, and spiritually by men who had a lot of power in the Jewish culture of that day, but that was nothing new. It had happened many years prior to that incident, as seen in some earlier Biblical stories.

In one of King David's lowest moments, he saw Bathsheba bathing on a roof top and was struck by her beauty. He instructed a servant to bring her to him, and he had sex with her which resulted in her getting pregnant. (2 Samuel 11:1-5). As king, his power was the highest in the land. By that time in his life, David apparently had come to believe his needs took precedence over everyone else's. Though he knew she was married to one of his loyal soldiers, that it was sin to have sex with another man's wife, and though he had other wives who could fulfill his sexual needs, he still chose to have sex with her. She probably believed she had no choice. Saying, "No," to the king might have been perilous, possibly resulting in her death, or at least, that may have been what she believed.

In another incident in the Bible (2 Samuel 13:1-20), David's son, Amnon fell in love with Tamar, his half-sister. He pretended to be ill and asked his father if Tamar could come and prepare food for him and feed him. His father granted his request. After Tamar prepared some bread, Amnon sent everyone from the room and propositioned his half-sister. She begged him to stop and even suggested they ask their father to let them marry, but he overpowered and raped her. She then so repulsed him he cast her aside with no regard for the scars she carried and the negative ramifications she lived with for the rest of her life.

These are just two stories in the Bible that illustrate how women could be used and abused by men back then.

By the time of Jesus, many years after King David and his son, not much had changed regarding the societal values for a woman. A woman was still seen as property by whatever male had charge of her life, whether her father, husband, brother, or adult son. She had no legal rights. If her father or husband died, she could not inherit anything from them. And because many women were uneducated and unskilled, it was difficult for a woman to support and protect herself if she had no male relative. Without family, becoming a beggar or prostitute were sometimes the only options available to a woman to be able to survive.

Jesus fully understood the struggles of women, the powerlessness they experienced, and the ways the culture allowed men to discount, use, abuse, and abandon them. He cared about their plight. Stories in the Gospels show that Jesus treated women like whole human beings made in the image of God, not as pieces of property. Jesus was so spiritually intuitive he could tell the deeper truth behind someone's words and actions. He knew what was in each person's heart and mind.

In his saying, "Go, and leave your life of sin," Jesus was not just another man shaming this woman. He didn't blame her and tell her it was all her fault as these men had done. But neither did he ignore something within her that prompted her to engage sexually with a man who was not her husband. If she had been raped or forced into sex against her will, Jesus would have known. He knew that was not fully the truth or Jesus would not have pointed to some sin in her life. Along with needing protection and safety he knew there was something within her that needed to be cleaned out and renewed to experience the fullness of what God wanted for her. He offered that to her when he said he did not condemn her yet invited her to leave her life of sin.

No doubt, she was extremely grateful Jesus rescued her from an excruciating death. But it was his acceptance, compassion, and truth that allowed her to be released from her old identity and to embrace "precious treasure" as her new identity.

WHAT CAN WE LEARN FROM THIS STORY?

Jesus cared deeply about this woman who experienced a devastating trauma. He also fully understands and cares about how any similar trauma affects us today.

(Warning: the next section could trigger some painful memories and emotions if you have ever experienced any kind of sexual violence.)

Sexual abuse and assault are some of the most traumatizing and humiliating experiences a woman can have. Through the years I've worked with many women (and some men) who carried shame, hurt, or anger because of the abuse or rape they endured as a child, teenager, or young adult. It affected their sense of self and safety. Many of them believed it was their fault or there was something wrong with them. Some had difficulty trusting again. All felt disregarded, disrespected, and sometimes discarded.

Sadly, sexual assault occurs every day. According to RAINN (Rape, Abuse, and Incest Network), "Every 74 seconds, an American is sexually assaulted," and "every nine minutes, that victim is a child." RAINN also indicates, "One in 9 girls and one in 20 boys under the age of 18 experience sexual abuse or assault." Additionally, "82 percent of all victims under 18 are female."[3] The negative effects of sexual abuse or assault can be long lasting.

The "Me Too" movement, which began in 2006, suddenly went viral on social media in 2017. It exposed ways numerous women have been sexually used and abused. Many women came forward to acknowledge they experienced it as a child or teenager. Some said as adults they'd been required to have sex with someone in authority over them to keep or advance in their job, or they were sidelined because of their refusal. It's not surprising to hear of this happening in the worlds of Hollywood and big business, but unfortunately, abuse wasn't limited to just those places.

An article in Sojourners magazine noted that between 2004 and 2024, forty Catholic organizations in the United States, including some dioceses, filed for bankruptcy protection through Chapter 11. It's in response to the many lawsuits accusing priests of abusing children.[4]

In some evangelical churches, pastors or other church staff have been accused of sexually abusing girls or women in their churches. Boz Tchividjian, a former States Attorney in Florida, the grandson of Billy Graham, and the founder of GRACE (Godly Response to Abuse in the Christian Environment) says sexual abuse in evangelical churches now "rivals the Catholic Church scandal of the early 2000's."[5]

This information is truly sobering and sad. Part of that sadness comes from knowing that kind of trauma fuels lies a woman might believe about herself for years: *Responsibility Lies* of "It's my fault." *Capability Lies* of, "How could I have been so stupid to trust or let this happen?" *Acceptability Lies* of, "I'm dirty. I'm trash." *Vulnerability Lies* of, "I'm not safe. I'm powerless. God wasn't there." *Possibility Lies* of, "I can no longer freely live my life." These experiences can prompt us to lose our truest self and begin to hide from God and from others. They can also hold us back from fully living the life God wants us to live.

Have you ever had an experience in which you were used, abused, or betrayed?
What lies have you believed about yourself because of it?
How much does it affect your life today?

No one is seen as trash or discardable to Jesus. He did not view this woman that way. He responded to her as someone worthy of being seen, heard, cared about, protected, and healed. He sees each of us the same way, too, no matter what we have done or what has been done to us.

Through this story Jesus gives us a glimpse of the grace and love that God the Father has for each of us. No matter how we have sinned or have been sinned against. No matter who has used, rejected or discarded us. No matter how much we've been treated as trash.

Jesus longs to go with us through whatever situation we find ourselves in, whether because of our own sin or someone's sin against us. He wants to give us his strength and guidance to face whatever is scary and humiliating. He longs for us to turn to him when we need protection. He wants to either rescue us from these kinds of circumstances or heal us from their impact.

The picture God holds in His mind of each of us is the one He first envisioned of us before we were conceived. He sees who we really are underneath whatever traumas we may have experienced and lies we have believed. He treasures each of us no matter what has happened to us. He wants to heal us from the impact of something so devastating.

Have you ever had an experience in which you were treated as though you were junk, trash, or discardable?

Just as Jesus never condemned this woman, he never condemns us, no matter how many rules we have broken, or how far we have strayed from the path he desires us to be on.

Though the Law of Moses was important to Jesus, he was not just about rules and regulations. Rather, he was about a balance of truth and grace. His grace and compassion for this woman, even in her sin, was beyond anything she had ever experienced. Because of his deep love for her, he wanted her to stop engaging in anything that separated her from God. He wanted her to sin no more not because he was trying to control her, but rather, because he wanted her to experience the best God had for her.

In the same way, Jesus is never surprised or condemning when we go off track and make a mess of our lives. He always welcomes us back into the embrace of his love. His grace is beyond anything we can imagine. He forgives us. He wants to heal us from the pain we've gone through. And he invites us to become free of the lies we came to believe because of abuse or betrayal. He wants to replace those lies with his truth about us. He longs for us to discover who he originally created us to be before we ever sinned or were sinned against. He invites us to move from seeing ourselves as "trash" and to embrace "precious treasure" as our truest identity.

What words describe how you see your truest identity?

PRAYER

Thank you, Jesus, that you care very much about the plight of women. You know and care if we have been used, abused, or betrayed in any way. Thank you for being willing to come right into the middle of our deepest pain and humiliation and to love us anyway. Thank you for willingly exchanging our shame for a crown of beauty.

Lord, Jesus, thank you that your grace covers all our sin. Thank you for having already paid the price for any of our failings, any of our mistakes, anything we've done that was not in alignment with who you are or who you desire us to be. Thank you for providing a way to repent and bring all our shame and brokenness to you. Thank you that when God, the Father, looks at us, He sees us through the lens of you and your perfection, no matter how imperfect we are.

Jesus, for any woman who is in a relationship with someone who is using, abusing, or betraying her, or with anyone who tramples on who she is as a person, please give her your wisdom and strength to choose the right path. Provide concrete, practical resources so she can live in safety and dignity. Also please send an army of angels to surround her and protect her, her property, and the people she loves.

Lord, give her your wisdom to recognize early on in a relationship someone who might mistreat her in this manner. Give her your strength to walk away from that. Empower her to trust that you know who is best for her and will direct her if she opens her eyes, ears, mind, and heart to you.

Jesus, for any woman who has ever been used, abused, or betrayed, please hold her hand as you walk through those painful memories with her. Set her free from the lies she came to believe about herself, about others, and about you in all of it.

Thank you that, in you, we are free to fully embrace the wonderful truth that we are not trash or junk. In fact, we are precious treasures made in your image. Thank you that you desire to take up residence within our heart and mind so your Spirit will be a stream of living water that never dries up, that always flows abundantly.

QUESTIONS FOR PERSONAL REFLECTION AND GROUP SHARING

1. What glimpses of the heart, mind, and character of Jesus do you see in this story?
2. Have you ever been in any relationship where you felt like you were devalued, used, abused, or betrayed by another person? If so, what was happening?
3. What gets in the way of you believing God sees you as a precious treasure? How hard is it for *you* to believe you are a precious treasure?
4. It's common for people who experienced abuse or trauma to believe negative things about themselves, others, or even about God. If you had that kind of experience, what negative things feel true even if you know they aren't true?
   A. Lies about you and your self-worth.
   B. Lies about other people.
   C. Lies about God.

5. If you've suffered abuse or betrayal, what kind of support and encouragement did you receive from people around you at the time? Or what kind of support and encouragement did you *need* to receive? What acceptance, support and encouragement do you need right now?
6. These kinds of painful situations often impact our faith. If you have experienced abuse or trauma, how did that impact your faith? Did it cause you to doubt, or to draw closer to God?
7. If you have experienced healing, what helped you to heal?

AN EXERCISE TO TRY

Activating the Pathways in Your Brain Associated with Feeling Safe and Peaceful:

Because it can feel uncomfortable, even scary and embarrassing to recall a memory when you were used or abused, it's beneficial to be able to, first, reconnect with a memory of a time when you felt peaceful. This helps prepare you to work on any painful memories. This exercise helps you activate pathways in your brain already associated with feeling peaceful, calm, and safe. It can make it easier to work on healing painful memories. While it does not solve a problem, it can help you develop a way to remain grounded and centered as you do any future healing work:

Begin by focusing on your breathing, slowly inhaling through your nose, and exhaling through your mouth. Let your abdominal muscles relax to allow the air to go down deep to the floor of your lungs. It might feel like you are breathing into your pelvis. If you struggle with this kind of breathing, it's much easier to do it lying down. This kind of breath facilitates a better balance between oxygen and carbon dioxide in your body and is the first strategy for getting calmer. Do at least three to five breaths in this manner.

As you relax, ask Jesus to take you back to any memory where you felt peaceful and calm. Where were you in that positive memory and what was happening? Were you alone in a beautiful place in nature or with a group of people doing something enjoyable? What do you recall seeing? What sounds do you remember hearing? Are there smells or tastes associated with this memory? What do you recall feeling in your body? What do you remember feeling emotionally? As you continue to breathe slowly and deeply, allow the peacefulness of the memory to grow as you continue to recall it for a little while. As you remember this memory in detail, the pathways in your brain associated with it will get activated and you'll probably notice yourself feeling calmer.

Once you have the memory clearly in your mind, slowly and gently tap on each of your shoulders, your right hand on your left shoulder and your left hand on your right shoulder, six to eight times. You can do several sets of tapping. Another name for this is the "Butterfly Hug," which is a tool for self-soothing and emotional regulation. (You can learn more about this method at www.tappingassociation.com) Only tap briefly as you recall the peacefulness of the memory. If it starts to not feel peaceful, discontinue the exercise.

A note about therapy

If you have ever experienced any kind of sexual abuse or assault, there are powerful kinds of therapies today that can help you release any lingering pain or shame attached to those memories. EMDR (Eye Movement Desensitization and Reprocessing) and EFT (Emotional Freedom Technique) are two kinds of therapies that do not require you to talk in detail about your experiences. They usually are faster and more effective than traditional "talk" therapy.

Eye Movement Desensitization and Reprocessing, or EMDR is a kind of psychotherapy that involves bilateral stimulation of the left and right brain. It is an evidence-based therapy that helps someone release the negative emotional charge they still carry from a trauma they experienced. It is particularly helpful when someone experiences symptoms of Post Traumatic Stress Disorder. You can learn more about this therapy at www.EMDR.com

Another helpful tool is called *Immanuel Prayer,* which is basically a three-way prayer conversation between you, a facilitator, and God. It's a way of gaining God's perspective on the truth of who you are, even in the memories of times in your life that took you away from your truest identity in Christ. The website listed in the resources section at the back of this book offers a list of people in the United States and around the world who are trained in using Immanuel Prayer.

If you have not yet experienced healing and freedom in your life from something that has kept you in chains, I encourage you to find someone trained in Immanuel Prayer or a therapist trained in EMDR to help you move towards greater freedom in your life. Some Christian therapists are trained in both.

SIX
A Desperate Woman
MATTHEW 15: 21 – 28, MARK 7:24 - 30

THAT FIRST MONTH of Baby Richie's life, his mom, Mickey, knew something wasn't right about him. It seemed like such an effort for him to nurse, as though he was too tired to keep trying to take in breast milk. He didn't gain weight. His lips had a bluish tinge.

"Something seems wrong, but I'm a new mom. Maybe I worry too much. Or maybe I'm doing something wrong," Mickey thought.

Her worst fears were confirmed when she took him for his one-month check-up. Richie's pediatrician suspected something was wrong with the baby's heart. After going through a battery of tests, he was diagnosed with congenital heart disease. That began a long journey of years of numerous surgeries and other medical procedures that included many hospitalizations. Those were agonizing years for his mom as she cared for Richie while watching his health decline. Not knowing if he would live, she was desperate for God to heal her precious little one.

In Matthew 15:21-28 and Mark 7:24-30, we read about another mom who was also desperate for her child to be healed. Since many illnesses back then were attributed to demons, she believed her daughter was demon possessed. The text doesn't tell us her daughter's symptoms or how long she'd been suffering. But the mom's bold request and persistence might suggest Jesus was this frantic mother's last hope.

THE STORY

Jesus traveled through the Jewish region of Galilee with his disciples while he taught about the Kingdom of God, healed the sick, and required demons to leave. One day, though, he decided to leave that area and travel to Tyre and Sidon, two cities outside of Jewish territory in the region known as Phoenicia.

How interesting that Jesus chose to visit a Gentile area. It was not a place most Jews would visit if they sought to keep all the Mosaic ceremonial laws. Anything belonging to or touched by a Gentile was seen as unclean. Out of a fear of being defiled, most Jews of Jesus' day avoided Gentile territories.

That was not what Jesus believed, though. In Mark 7:24, we learn Jesus visited a house in that area but apparently did not want people to know he was there. Perhaps he needed a rest from the constant attention he received in Israel and he decided to go where he was not so well known. Or maybe he knew that a mom and a little girl there needed him. His presence didn't stay secret for long.

News of Jesus' arrival traveled quickly and soon a local woman found him. She was a Greek woman born in Syrian Phoenicia, so in Mark's version of the story she is called the Syro-Phoenician woman. Mark was writing to a Roman audience, so those readers would have identified the woman by the name of the territory in the Roman Empire where she lived.

In Matthew's version of the story, he identifies her as a Canaanite woman because Matthew was addressing a Jewish audience. Those readers would have identified the woman by their shared history.[1] The Canaanites were some of the Indigenous people living in the land prior to the Israelites settling in what came to be known as "the Promised Land." As the Jews began to make that land their home, not surprisingly they clashed with the people who already lived there. Hence, there was a long-standing animosity between the Israelites and the Canaanites. While they often saw each other as enemies, by the time of Jesus they had one thing in common—the Roman Empire ruled over both territories. Still, because the Canaanites were Gentiles, the Jewish people of Jesus' day believed the people of Tyre and Sidon were dirty, unrighteous heathens and dogs.

Why did this woman search for Jesus?

Because as a mother she was desperate. She believed her young daughter was held captive by a demonic spirit. No doubt, Jesus' reputation as a healer who could release someone from the chains of demonic oppression had preceded his visit to that town. This dedicated mom hoped her daughter would finally be healed and set free by Jesus.

"Lord, Son of David, have mercy on me. My daughter suffers terribly from demon possession." (Matthew 15:22)

We don't know how old her daughter was, what symptoms she experienced, how long she'd suffered, and how it affected her life. We are simply told the woman had a young daughter with an "unclean spirit." Since people of that day knew nothing about modern medicine or psychology, illnesses or unusual behaviors were believed to be caused by a demonic spirit. Medically, it's possible her daughter had an illness, such as epilepsy. Or perhaps she was born healthy but developed a disease that took away her ability to see, hear, talk, or walk. Whatever the reason she was seen as having a demonic spirit, this mom was determined to do everything she could to help her daughter become healed and free.

The woman continued to beg, "Please, help my daughter."

But Jesus just ignored her. His disciples likely thought that was the proper way to respond to her, so they also ignored her. They knew it was against society's rules for a man and a woman to talk to each other in public, so they didn't interact with her.

But they finally got tired of her persistence and said to Jesus, "Send her away, for she keeps crying out after us." (Matthew 15:23)

What transpired next is one of the most confusing, confounding stories about Jesus in the whole New Testament. Jesus responded differently to this woman than anyone else who sought his help. Jesus, who would help anyone who had faith enough to ask for it, just ignored her. No word. Nothing. Nada.

And then when he finally did speak, what a surprise.

"I was sent only to the lost sheep of Israel," he said. (Matthew 15:24)

What?

Why would Jesus say that to her? After all, he was the one who decided to go into a non-Jewish territory. And it's not like she was the first Gentile who ever sought help from him. Other people who were not Jewish had also asked for his help and he readily gave it: The Samaritan woman at the well (John 4:1-42). The Roman Centurion whose son was dying (Matthew 8:5-13). The demon-possessed man who lived among the tombs in the country of the Gerasenes (Mark 5:1-20). A deaf man with a speech impediment (Mark 7:31-37). None of these people were part of "the lost sheep of Israel," so why would Jesus respond this way to her?

It gets worse. She came and knelt in front of Jesus and begged for his help again. In response, it seems Jesus now also humiliated her.

"It is not right to take the children's bread and toss it to their dogs." (Matthew 15:26)

If you were called a "dog," what would that mean to you? As a woman, how would you respond? Dogs were not valued by the Jewish culture of that time. In fact, the word, "dog" was often used in a derisive way towards anyone not a Jew. It seems like Jesus demeaned this woman. What he said even sounded racist.

But is that *really* what's going on?

I believe Jesus spoke aloud the thoughts circling round in the disciples' minds. His words reflected their unspoken thoughts. He knew what they believed and the judgments they made about this persistent Gentile woman. I wonder if perhaps Jesus kept quiet to give his disciples a chance to respond to her. Would any one of them try to help her? Would anyone express compassion? Would they respond to her out of the cultural traditions that prohibited a man and a woman from talking to each other in public? Would they respond to her out of the racial bigotry and prejudices the Jews of that day held towards Gentiles? Or would they respond to her out of the actions and words Jesus had modeled for them with the Samaritan woman at the well?

I've heard Bible teachers say Jesus' response to her was just a test of the woman's faith. I see it differently. I think this was a moment in time when Jesus tested the *disciples*. Maybe Jesus gave them an opportunity to demonstrate to him that they understood the bigger picture of his teachings—that he came to earth for all people, not just the people of Israel. Jesus knew he would eventually leave this earth and his disciples would continue his work. They would become leaders in a movement that would impact the entire world. Had they made progress towards that?

Their response to this woman would show Jesus how much they understood and embraced his teachings about who was invited to be a part of the Kingdom of God. To effectively and authentically carry out the "great commission" he knew he was going to give them in the future, the disciples would need to be able to step outside the cultural prejudices and bigotries of that day. They would need to be able to care for all people regardless of race, culture, or gender.

If that was Jesus' intention, it seems the disciples failed the test. They were not yet ready to live out Jesus' future commission to them of, "Go and make disciples of *all* nations, baptizing them in the name of the Father, Son, and Holy

Spirit, and teaching them to obey everything I have taught you."

In fact, sometime before this story took place, we read in Mark 6:7-13, Jesus sent out his disciples two by two to teach and heal. Jesus specifically instructed them to *not* go to the Gentiles or Samaritans. Maybe this experience was like an internship or a practicum where the disciples would get to practice the things they would be called to do once Jesus returned to Heaven. But when he gave them that specific instruction to not go to certain people, maybe Jesus knew they were not yet ready to let go of the prejudices of their day towards anyone not male and not Jewish.

So, if the woman interpreted Jesus' words to her as demeaning, she did not let it interfere with her goal of getting help for her daughter. As she continued to kneel in front of him when he said, "It is not right to take the children's food and toss it to the dogs," she quickly answered him, "Yes, Lord, but even the dogs eat the crumbs that fall from their master's table." (Matthew 15:27)

Good answer!

Jesus' response was a resounding, "Woman, you have great faith. Your request is granted." (Matthew 15:28)

What a joyous occasion it must have been when this mom returned home and discovered her daughter had been completely healed. She was now free to live her life. Relief and gratitude must have flooded this mom's heart and mind! I wonder what their family did to celebrate that momentous occasion?

No doubt this encounter with Jesus changed the trajectory of this woman's life. Rather than a life devoted to the care of a sick child becoming progressively sicker and weaker, she now had a healthy child. Instead of perhaps holding her child's hand as she took her last breath, this mom got to witness her daughter grow up. Maybe she got to see her daughter get married. Perhaps she got to be a part of the births of her grandchildren and help them grow up, too. She likely would have shared this story with her grandkids, telling them how Jesus healed their mom and changed her own life.

By the way, little Richie, whom you met in the beginning of this chapter, went on to live with heart disease for a remarkable 30 years. Though he couldn't play sports or run like other kids, his life was a blessing to his family and everyone who knew him.

WHAT CAN WE LEARN FROM THIS STORY?

Jesus saw who this woman really was, beyond the cultural, ethnic, and gender stereotypes of his day. He saw her heart and mind. He knew her truest self. He responds to each of us in the same way today.

He didn't put people in boxes like, "enemy," "less than," or "unlovable." He willingly associated with people the religious leaders saw as dirty, evil, unrighteous dogs, never judging them as unworthy.

Jesus does not respond to us, either, out of any negative beliefs society might hold about our race, gender, or culture. He sees beyond all that into our hearts and minds and loves us for who we truly are. He desires for us to become free to be who God the Father created and designed us to be. He sees each of us as a person made in the image of God, worthy of love and respect. He knows the Father had a picture in his mind of each of us before we were ever conceived. He planned for you to be you. Think of the significance of that. Really let it sink in: you were *designed* to be you regardless of how society might view you.

> *Have you ever felt judged or mistreated because of someone's stereotypical beliefs regarding your gender, race, or culture?*

What is the truth about you that Jesus wants you to believe and live out?

Just like this woman didn't receive an immediate answer to her requests, sometimes we also need to wait for an answer.

Have you ever felt ignored by Jesus? Like he didn't hear your prayers or didn't care what you were going through? Sometimes he responds quickly to us but sometimes, he is silent for a while, as he was with this woman. He doesn't always answer our requests immediately but that does not mean he isn't there or doesn't care. He sees the bigger picture of our lives and knows our waiting to get an answer to our requests might be an important part of his plans for us. There can be benefits to waiting we don't immediately recognize.

If it ever seemed like your prayers were not heard or they were ignored, what did you come to believe about God? How did that impact you?

The disciples were irritated with this woman's persistence, but Jesus was not. He respected her tenacity and her willingness to repeatedly bring her needs to him. He also respects our perseverance when we bring our needs to him.

This woman disregarded the cultural expectations of that time about what a woman should or should not do in public. The disciples appear to look down on and judge her for that. Apparently, Jesus didn't hold to the idea, though, that a woman should remain quiet and not have a voice. This story seems to indicate that Jesus believed it was okay for a woman to have a voice and to use it persistently if needed.

Have you ever had an experience of either not being able to have a voice, or you were judged negatively when you used your voice to express your needs, wants, and ideas?

All of us had a mother and some of us are mothers. This story reminds us that good mothers aren't always polite or demure. Sometimes they need to be persistent and strong. We can learn about mothering our children better as we study this woman who never gave up.

Remember the children's story, "Goldilocks and the Three Bears?" When Goldilocks entered the bears' home while they were away, she tried the porridge in all three bowls on the table and found them either too hot, too cold, or just right. She sat in the three chairs belonging to each bear and then lay down in their three beds, but they were either too hard, too soft, or just right. Well, some mothers are like that...too hot, too cold, too hard, too soft, and some mothers are "just right."

What kind of mother do you think the woman in this story was? We can assume some things about her from both stories in Matthew and Mark. First, she loved her daughter fiercely, so much that she was willing to break cultural norms and approach a man who was a stranger to ask for help. She wasn't afraid to advocate for her daughter. She believed her daughter should have a chance at life and happiness, and she did everything in her power to fight for that. She also had faith. She believed Jesus cared and that he had the power to heal. She wouldn't have continued to ask for help even when he seemed to ignore her if she didn't believe in the healing power of Jesus. This mother was one who was "just right." And being "just right" sometimes depends on the situation. Sometimes a mom needs to be a strong advocate for her daughter.

That didn't mean she didn't believe some lies, though. Certainly, *Vulnerability Lies* of, "My daughter's life is not safe. She is possessed by a demon," and "She is going to die," felt true to her. From Jesus' perspective, those beliefs were not true. Thankfully, she apparently did not believe *Capability Lies*, like, "I'm not capable of asking for help for my daughter." Nor did she believe *Acceptability Lies* of "I'm not worthy of help."

If you are a mother, whether your kids are young or older, what are ways you are like this woman? What kind of mother are you: too hot, too cold, too hard, too soft, or just right? What might your kids say about that? What lies do/did you believe as a mother? And what messages do you give them now through your words, actions, or attitudes that help them embrace their truest identity in Jesus? Or were there messages you gave them that interfered with them believing the truth of who they are in God's eyes?

If you are a mother, what ways do you seek to help your kids learn and believe the truth of who they are from God's perspective?

This mother also teaches us about how to love the parts of ourselves that need to receive a "just right" kind of love.

Look again at what this mother gave to her daughter: acceptance, love, and advocacy. Her daughter was so important to her she never stopped fighting for her. She gave the best she had to her daughter. In which ways was your mother like or not like that? What did you receive from your mother? Was she too hot, too cold, too hard, too soft, or just right? What messages did you receive from her through her words, actions, or attitudes that were beneficial? Were there messages you received that were not helpful and fueled lies you still believe? How has that affected your life?

Years ago, I led an all-day seminar called *Adult Daughters and Mothers: Managing Your Most Complicated Relationship*. About twenty women participated. Surprisingly, only two of the women were mothers of adult daughters. They both came with a desire to restore broken relationships with their daughters. They were able to acknowledge the mistakes they had made and regrets they had about the ways they had not been the kind of mothers their daughters needed them to be.

The rest were adult daughters who came seeking three things:

- How to deal more effectively with their own mother who was still alive but was not the kind of mother they needed or wanted
- How to mother their own child in a healthier, more accepting and affirming way than they had been mothered
- How to heal from whatever "mother wounds" they carried because they had not been mothered in a healthy and accepting way.

All of them wanted to feel more worthy of love and to be loved, to feel more acceptable and be accepted for who they were, even if they hadn't received the kind of mothering that facilitated those things.

At the seminar, I introduced these women to a strategy that helped them begin to heal and develop greater resilience. Participants learned how to give acceptance, love, nurture, and truth to the younger parts of themselves who missed out on those things.

You, too, can learn how to use this powerful tool.

They first learned how to identify the wise, strong, compassionate "Self," or the "Adult Ally" within themselves. You also can do that by, first, remembering times in your life when you responded to someone (or even an animal) with compassion, wisdom, and strength. Recall any sights, sounds, smells, tastes, body sensations, and emotions that are part of those memories. You can do that either through journaling about it or visualizing it. This can activate pathways in your brain associated with feeling wise, strong, and compassionate.

Next, the participants learned how to use that wise, strong, compassionate Self to "go back in time" to a memory that still held shame, fear, hurt, or anger. You likely have a part of you like that, and you can use it to provide what the younger parts of you needed but didn't receive…acceptance, love, nurture, encouragement, truth, and maybe rescue and protection. Because our unconscious is a literalist, an intense imagery exercise will be recorded in your brain as if it is an actual experience.

This is a powerful exercise by itself, but as a follower of Jesus, we also want his perspective of us. So, you can ask Jesus what lies you came to believe in that memory. Once they have been highlighted, ask Jesus if what you came to believe in that memory matches his truth for you. Then ask him to bring his love, truth, and peace into that memory and set you free from the power of the lies.

What did you need to receive as a child that you missed out on? If it were miraculously possible to travel back to a time in your life when you needed something emotionally, what memory would you go to and what would you give yourself?

This is not an easy concept to understand so allow me to give you an example of that from my own life. My mom adored babies and was a wonderful mom to all her babies. But she didn't really like 2-year-olds. I heard her say a number of times, "When a child turns two and starts engaging in 2-year-old behavior, I would just as soon pass them on to someone else to raise." Not surprisingly, she had a baby every two years, and I was the oldest of five kids. While I have no conscious memories of the loss of that close, nurturing relationship with my mom at age two, it fueled in me insecurity, anxiety, and a sense of "I'm not good enough." *Acceptability Lies* got installed in my heart and mind at a very young age.

As an adult, one day I was doing some healing work around the insecurity and anxiety I felt. An image suddenly came to mind of a little two-year-old girl who was sad and felt left out of the wonderful moments of nurture between her mother and her baby brother. When I discovered that little girl inside my mind it was like finding a secret door to a hidden room in the basement of my life. I opened that door, and in my imagination, there was that little two-year-old girl sitting in dim light on the cold floor hugging her knees to her chest, feeling sad and alone. I instantly felt such compassion for her. Using my imagination, I brought her out into the light, held and rocked her, and told her how much I loved her and how deeply sorry I was that she experienced losing out when her baby brother was born. I told her things like, "I see you. I hear you. You are wanted. You are enough. I will always love you and be with you. I will never leave you."

That was a profound turning point for me. It helped me to love and nurture that little two-year-old girl in myself and, later, other parts of myself who also needed acceptance, love, comfort, and approval. The more I practiced this exercise with various "parts" of myself, I was amazed at how much it eased the anxiety, insecurity, and my sense of not being "good enough." It allowed me to *feel* loved and worthy of love instead of just *knowing* it with my mind. It also helped me embrace God's truth of who I was: a cherished, treasured child of God.

As I began to comfort and love that little girl inside, something else profound happened. I experienced compassion and love for my mom. She, too, had a mother who pushed her away when she was two years old, partly because Mom had an older sister who died at age two. Her mother's grief and sadness had gotten in the way of her being the mother my mom needed, which I believe interfered with my mom being the mother I needed as a young child.

"Re-mothering" yourself through visualization, journaling, and other exercises can be a powerful tool to help the "younger parts" of yourself begin to feel accepted, loved, valued, and welcomed. It can calm anxiety, heal hurts, and release shame and anger. It also brings you into greater alignment with what Jesus thinks of and feels toward you.

PRAYER

Lord, Jesus, you know the ways each of us were mothered and the impact that had on our lives, both positively and negatively. Some of us had a mother who was not able to be the kind of mom we needed her to be. So, please help us heal. Give us a picture of how you see us and remind us often that as your child, we are so worthy of being loved, are lovable, and are incredibly loved, regardless of what we received from our mothers. Fill up any empty places inside us with you. Mend our broken hearts. And please help us understand what happened in our mom's life that may have interfered with her being the mom we needed her to be. Show us how to forgive.

Holy Spirit, for any woman reading this whose mother is still alive, please help her mom understand how much you accept and love her and how much you accept and love her daughter. If she has truly done something harmful to her daughter, please lead her to recognize and own her mistakes, make changes, and seek forgiveness. Please give her awareness that you want to bless her, heal her, and if possible, move her and her daughter towards having a safe and satisfying relationship with each other.

Jesus, you know the fear a mom feels when her child is dangerously ill or dealing with something disabling, is engaging in behaviors with possible harmful consequences, or is even fighting an addiction. For any mom reading this who experiences that, please come into the middle of that fear. Flood her with your peace and compassion. Allow her and her child to feel your embrace, comfort, support, and strength. I also pray for complete healing physically, mentally, emotionally, and spiritually for her child.

Lord, you know the women out there who are tired and

overwhelmed, who struggle with difficult things, like financial or job stresses, relationship turmoil, major losses, recovery from something catastrophic, or who deal with prejudices from others. Please provide whatever resources they need to get through all that. Make your presence known to them in a very concrete and tangible way. Allow them to experience your peace, rest, and strength. Surround and cover them with your love and blessing.

QUESTIONS FOR PERSONAL REFLECTION AND GROUP SHARING

1. What do you notice about the heart, mind, and character of Jesus in this story?
2. If you ever experienced a time of feeling desperate and needing help, what was happening and how old were you? How did help come?
3. If you have ever experienced a sense of being ignored, not listened to, or disregarded, how did that affect you emotionally and spiritually?
4. If anyone ever responded to you in a hurtful way out of their own prejudice and bigotry, what happened and how did it affect you?
5. What "lies" about yourself, others, or God got planted in your heart and mind during any of those times? How true do they still feel today?
6. What do you recall about the mothering you received? Too hot or too cold? Too hard or too soft? Or "just, right"? If your mom was not a "just right" mom, was there someone else in your life who "mothered" you?
7. If not, who is someone that illustrated the actions and words of a "just right" kind of mom, like, the mother of your best friend, or a neighbor or

teacher? If no one comes to your mind, you can ask Jesus to give you a picture of a "mother figure" who can give love, acceptance, comfort, nurture, and support to the "parts" of yourself who need to receive that.

AN EXERCISE TO TRY

There is a wonderful story in Mark 10:13-16 that tells of a time when a group of mothers brought their children to Jesus for a blessing. What might it be like if you could imagine being one of those mothers and do one of the following:

1. Either imagine bringing your child (at whatever age you choose) to Jesus for a blessing.
2. Or imagine bringing a younger part of yourself (at whatever age you were) to Jesus for a blessing.

If you are open to doing this exercise, find a comfortable place where you can be alone for a while without interruptions.

Read Mark 10:13-16. Ask Jesus to show you anything important for you to know.

Take a few slow, deep breaths, being aware of where the breath goes when it goes to the center of you.

Briefly recall a time when you felt relaxed and calm, like being on the beach or at a peaceful vacation spot. Recall what you saw, heard, smelled, tasted, felt in your body, and felt emotionally. Let yourself unwind and relax.

Now imagine what it might be like for you and your child to walk down that road with that group of moms and their kids:

What might the weather be like?

What might the terrain/landscape be like, such as, a dusty road, rockiness, the Jordan River or the Sea of Galilee, grassy hills?

What sounds might you hear?

What smells or tastes might be present?

What possible tactile experiences would you be experiencing, such as the wind on your skin, the dust of the road on your feet if you were barefoot or wearing sandals, or the warm sun?

See the picture in your mind about what happens when the moms and kids get close to where Jesus was teaching. Visualize how the disciples responded to your group.

Imagine Jesus' response to the disciples and what he said to them.

How might you and the other moms think and feel about that? And the kids?

Now imagine Jesus' response to each child as he gives them a blessing. How does Jesus respond to the child you brought to him?

What does Jesus say?

What is his tone of voice?

What expression is on Jesus' face?

In what way does Jesus use safe, gentle touch with the child you have brought for a blessing?

What is it like to be enveloped by Jesus' love and compassion?

Once Jesus has blessed the child you have brought to him, how does that child respond?

Allow yourself to enjoy the sights and sounds of the day one more time, and when you are ready, come back into the present time and place.

SEVEN

Two Different Women

LUKE 10:38-42; JOHN 11:1-55; JOHN 12:1-10

My younger sister, Brenda, and I, born five years apart, were different from each other in temperament, giftedness, and approach to life. School came easily to her. She was always at the top of her class and effortlessly got all A's on her report cards. Teachers loved having her in their classes because she was bright, studious, dependable, and mature for her age. I was not a bad student, but I had to work a lot harder than she did. We both loved to read but we even approached that differently. In the summer she would retreat to her bedroom, reading all afternoon, while I would take my book outside, climb a tree, and spend the afternoon reading perched in its branches.

Brenda was gentle, accommodating, and a peace maker. I, on the other hand, could be a little bossy. My being the oldest of five and her being the middle child probably influenced that. Brenda didn't want to offend or hurt anyone, so she was careful with what she said and how she said it. I had a bit of a "smart mouth" at home, which got me into trouble on occasion.

Brenda began writing as a teenager, expressing the longings of her soul through her incredible poetry, which displayed wisdom way beyond her years. She also loved to draw and paint. I didn't start writing until I reached mid-life and my attempts at writing poetry sounded like a child's. The artistic gene also passed by me.

As we became adults our differences became more evident. She was a quiet, gentle, contemplative woman comfortable spending time in solitude. I was busy with lots of projects. She seemed to value "being" over "doing" but sometimes failed to take the necessary steps to complete projects she started. Sometimes I was so busy "doing" that I failed to take time to slow down and reflect. Despite our differences, we were best friends. I loved her dearly. Spending time with Brenda renewed my heart and soul.

In the New Testament we read about two sisters who were also quite different. One seemed to value "being" while the other one was more focused on "doing." Brenda was more like Mary, and I was definitely more like Martha.

THE STORY

Martha, Mary, and their brother Lazarus were dear friends of Jesus. We don't know how they met or how their friendship developed. In their home, Jesus and his disciples relaxed and found respite from the large crowds who eagerly followed him. Three stories in the Gospels tell of the friendship and love between Jesus and this family. We also see significant ways he responded to each sister. Let's explore each story:

> **Story 1: Luke 10:38-42**
> "How wonderful to see you again! Please come to our home and have dinner with Mary, Lazarus, and me," might have been the invitation given to Jesus and his traveling companions.

Jesus and his disciples had come to Bethany, two miles from Jerusalem and home of the three siblings. Showing hospitality was highly valued. It was considered a privilege to share a meal with a guest. How excited Martha must have been for their home to be honored by Jesus' presence.

Planning a dinner party for over thirteen guests took time and organization, though. Martha probably made a quick survey of available foods in their pantry. Maybe she went out to her garden to pick vegetables and fruit. Did she slaughter a lamb or make a trip to the market to purchase meat? How long did it take to roast that meat over a fire? Did she grind grain and knead dough to make bread? How long did it take the bread to rise and bake? None of these activities would have been easy or quick, especially with no modern conveniences. Martha probably jumped into "doing" mode as she considered all that needed to be done. Such an event would likely have taxed even the most skilled, organized hostess.

As guests entered the home they were greeted with a kiss on the cheek and the road's dust was washed from their feet. Perhaps this was Mary's responsibility since Martha was overseeing the meal preparation. Martha probably assumed Mary would help her after finishing those tasks.

Apparently, Mary lost track of time as she listened to Jesus. His words grabbed her ears and then her heart and mind. She forgot about her sister making a meal for their guests. Perhaps as she sat at Jesus' feet her imagination opened to a world far different than what the religious leaders of that day taught. Maybe the younger sister caught an exciting glimpse of what life would be like when the Kingdom of God fully came into being. She opened to the idea that Jesus was the promised one, the Messiah. Being so caught up in what Jesus was saying, she thought of nothing else. Meanwhile, Martha really did need help. No doubt she had calculated the time she wanted to serve the meal and how long preparations would take with Mary's help. As Martha did the tasks she'd anticipated Mary would do, she became impatient, then irritated. Perhaps that incident tapped into some lies she believed:

"Why am I always the responsible one? I don't get to just sit and rest. Can't she see how hard I'm working? You'd think she'd recognize how important it is to serve our honored guests in a timely manner. Come on, Mary. Read my mind. Get in here now!"

What lies do you think Martha believed? She may have made judgments like, "Mary is not dependable. She's lazy. What's wrong with her that she doesn't see how hard I'm working while she is just sitting? Why do I have to take care of everything?" It sounds like Martha believed *Responsibility Lies*.

Rather than quietly going in and unobtrusively asking Mary to come and help, Martha let her emotions get the best of her. Finally, not able to stand it any longer Martha interrupted Jesus' teachings and blurted out, "Lord, don't you care that my sister has left me to do the work by myself? Tell her to help me!" (Luke 10:40)

What an awkward moment for everyone. Living in a culture oriented around honor and shame, Mary may have felt more humiliated than we could imagine today. Those present might have felt uncomfortable with this public critique. If Mary had previously been the recipient of Martha's judgments, it's possible her words triggered *Capability Lies* in Mary, like, "Why can't I stay focused? Why do I always mess up?" and *Acceptability Lies* of "There is something wrong with me. I must be stupid."

Jesus understood Martha's priorities and, no doubt, was grateful for the ways she wanted to serve him and his disciples. But having a delicious and filling meal was not his highest priority. The last thing he wanted was for his hosts to be so stressed over preparing a meal for him that they missed out on the nutritious spiritual food he offered.

The teacher answered by saying, "Martha, Martha, you are worried and upset about many things, but only one thing is needed. Mary has chosen what is better, and it will not be taken away from her." (vs. 41-42) Jesus didn't take offense at Martha's venting. He just gently let her know he valued *being with* them more than her *doing for* him.

Scripture doesn't say what happened next. Did Martha return to the kitchen to finish the meal, ashamed that Jesus called her out about her attitude? Did Mary, feeling guilty, hastily jump up and rush to help Martha? Or did Martha suddenly realize her frantic efforts weren't necessary? Maybe she realized Jesus was right, she relaxed and she sat down to enjoy his presence. Maybe she decided serving the meal at a certain time was not so important after all.

Perhaps this interaction with Jesus prompted Martha to evaluate what was most important in life and decide to make changes. Maybe she realized she was so focused on schedules, organization, and accomplishments that she often missed out on sweet fellowship with others and with God.

Maybe Jesus' approval of Mary confirmed to her there wasn't anything wrong with her even though she wasn't always organized, lost track of time, and occasionally irritated her sister. Perhaps it helped this younger sister embrace how she was designed by God. Maybe she realized the gifts she offered the world were valuable and beautiful, even if they were different from Martha's.

It's also important to remember that in that culture it was not acceptable for a woman to sit at the feet of a rabbi to learn. Only men did that. Maybe some of Martha's agitation was about Mary's disregard for proper etiquette. If so, Jesus upended that tradition. His acceptance of Mary sitting at his feet indicated it was acceptable to him for a woman to listen, learn, and ask questions even in the presence of men.

The meal did take place, probably later than Martha planned. By the end of it, though, everyone around that table likely felt satisfied physically and spiritually.

How much easier is it for you to "do" something for Jesus than to just spend time "being" with him?

Story 2: John 11:1-57
Martha sent word to Jesus, "Lord, the one you love is sick." (vs. 3)

Sometime after Jesus had visited the home of Mary, Martha, and Lazarus, he received word Lazarus was sick and near death. The sisters knew Jesus had healed many others, so they were desperate for him to come and heal their brother. Of course, they didn't want their beloved brother to suffer or lose his life. His death could also put them in a position of having no male family member to protect and support them as single women.

Clearly, Jesus had the capacity to heal Lazarus. He could have even spoken healing words from a distance and Lazarus would have been healed. That's probably what the disciples would have preferred he do when he said, "Let us go back to Judea." (vs. 7)

They reminded him, "But Rabbi, a short time ago the Jews tried to stone you, and you are going back there?" (vs. 8)

But healing Lazarus from a safe place was not what Jesus had in mind. Neither was returning to Bethany immediately. Instead, Jesus chose to delay their trip two days longer, perhaps for two reasons:

First, while not all the religious teachers believed this, some believed the soul could hang around for three days and even re-enter the body. After the third day, they believed it was impossible for the spirit to return to the body. Jesus knew people would be grateful if he healed Lazarus but bringing him back from the dead would be an even stronger confirmation that Jesus was truly the Son of God. Perhaps he chose to delay his trip so there would be no question in anyone's mind that a true miracle occurred when Lazarus returned to life.

Second, perhaps Jesus wanted to demonstrate his power over life and death as a foreshadowing of his own impending death and resurrection. Maybe he wanted to leave an indelible impression in everyone's mind that he had the power to come back from death after dying on a cross.

By the time Jesus and his followers reached Bethany, Lazarus had been dead for four days. What must it have been like for Martha and Mary to know Jesus healed many others but delayed coming to heal their brother? Did they anxiously watch the road each day for any sign of Jesus? Did they lose hope when he failed to come before Lazarus died? Were they confused or hurt at Jesus' late arrival? The sisters received word Jesus was approaching Bethany, so Martha hurried out to greet him.

"Lord, if you had been here, my brother would not have died." Was there a touch of anger and blame in her voice? "But even now I know God will give you whatever you ask of Him." (vs. 21-22)

Jesus answered, "Your brother will rise again." (vs. 23)

"I know he will rise in the resurrection on the last day." (vs. 24) It seems she believed Lazarus would rise again in the future but didn't grasp he could be returned to life that very day.

Jesus' answer might have sounded confusing at first. "I am the resurrection and the life. Those who believe in me, even though they die, will live, and everyone who lives and believes in me will never die. Do you believe this?" (vs. 25-26)

She answered, "Yes, Lord. I believe you are the Messiah, the Son of God, the one coming into the world." (vs. 27) In those few words, Martha revealed an open, trusting heart to Jesus.

Martha sent for Mary saying, "The teacher is here and is asking for you." (vs. 28)

Mary went quickly to Jesus and knelt at his feet. Like her sister, she also said, "If you had been here, my brother would not have died." (vs. 32)

Seeing their pain broke Jesus' heart. He wept even though he knew he planned to raise Lazarus from death. Jesus asked to be taken to the grave where Lazarus had been laid. Surprisingly, he instructed the disciples, "Take away the stone." (vs. 38)

Martha, always the practical one, immediately pointed out the hazard of that. "But Lord, by this time there is a bad odor, for he has been there four days." (vs. 40).

Jesus again reminded her, "Did I not tell you that if you believed, you would see the glory of God?" (vs. 40) So, the stone was rolled aside.

Jesus thanked God for hearing him and then loudly yelled, "Lazarus, come out!"

And that is what happened!

"Unbind him and let him go." (vs. 44) Loosen the grave wrappings. Release him. Set him free. The unfathomable, miraculous happened! Everyone present who witnessed it must have been beyond amazement and gratefulness. Right?

Well, actually, no. That wasn't the response of *everyone*.

Sadly, Jesus knew even a miracle of that magnitude would not convince the religious leaders of something they did not *want* to believe. He discerned they had closed their minds and hearts to the idea that he was the Messiah. In fact, some men who saw the miracle immediately left to go report it to the religious leaders.

An emergency meeting was quickly called by those leaders to discuss this situation they believed was getting out of hand.

"What do we do? This man does many miracles. If we just let this go on, everyone will follow him. And then what's going to happen? Well, I'll tell you what's going to happen. It's going to bring the Roman authorities down on us and our nation is going to be destroyed," is probably how the conversation went.

The High Priest, Caiaphas, then shared a cunning idea. "Is it too hard for you to see? It would be better for us if one man were to die for the people than for our whole nation to be destroyed." (John 11: 49-50, First Nations Version)

Many religious leaders believed the Messiah would come as a glorious, conquering military hero. They expected he would deliver the Jews from Roman oppression and restore the kingdom of Israel to its former strength and glory. "Make Israel

Great Again," was what they believed the true Messiah would do. But Jesus didn't fit the picture they carried in their mind of what the Messiah would say and do. They didn't understand Jesus was not seeking to establish an earthly kingdom but, rather, a heavenly kingdom. The religious leaders weren't taking any chances. They decided Jesus needed to die to save their nation.

From that day on they began to look for a time and place to capture Jesus, put him on trial, and sentence him to death. Jesus stopped walking openly among the crowds. He and his travel companions went to the village of Ephraim, near a wilderness area where he could more safely continue to teach his disciples until it was finally time to finish what he came to earth to do.

What grave is Jesus calling you out of?
What needs to be unbound, released, and set free in your life?

Story 3: John 12:1-11
"The Passover celebration will soon begin. Let's go to Bethany to visit our friends, Martha, Mary, and Lazarus one more time," Jesus might have said. And maybe he thought it but did not say it... "one last time."

Jesus was again in Bethany in the home of his three good friends but this time he was a "wanted" man. He had a target on his back because the religious leaders and Jewish authorities had ordered anyone who saw Jesus to report it to them. They believed he was a false prophet. Underneath their pretense of being righteous they were likely afraid the people would follow him, usurping their authority. Their jealousy blinded the leaders to what Jesus was really doing. There was no question in their minds: Jesus was a threat. So, they decided to arrest him, try him for blasphemy, and have the Roman authorities crucify him.

There was also no question in Jesus' mind regarding the

leaders' plans. He knew what he would face, should he return to the public eye. Still, he went to Bethany because he knew the completion of his mission was drawing near. As a human being, he might have dreaded the incredible suffering he knew he would endure, but as God, he never even considered not showing up.

Back in Bethany, Jesus was among people who loved and believed in him. This time the family gave a dinner to celebrate Lazarus' restored life. While Lazarus welcomed their guests, Martha did what she loved to do: extend hospitality and offer their guests food and warm fellowship.

Mary had other ideas, though. Besides Jesus, she might have been the only one who fully understood the impending danger Jesus faced, and the significance of what would take place soon. She knew he was going to die—be executed—and she prophetically spelled that out with her actions. Out of her deep love for Jesus, her teacher and friend, and in anticipation of her imminent grief, Mary poured a pound of pure nard on Jesus' feet and wiped them with her hair. Nard, an expensive perfume used by royalty, was also used to anoint a dead body for burial. As Mary knelt at Jesus' feet, she likely knew she was symbolically preparing his body for burial. She also knew she was anointing royalty—the King of Kings and Lord of Lords.

Not everyone understood Mary's love and devotion. Judas, one of the twelve disciples, expressed disgust with Mary's actions, judging them as wasteful.

"Why wasn't this perfume sold and the money given to the poor? It was worth a year's wages," he self-righteously proclaimed to the group. He really didn't care about the poor and even stole from the group's treasury. Judas may have also judged Mary for uncovering her hair and publicly touching Jesus, something only a prostitute would do.

But Jesus didn't allow Judas to get away with judging Mary. "Leave her alone. She bought it so that she might keep it for the day of my burial. You always have the poor with you, but you do not always have me." (vs. 7-8)

What was going on in Mary's heart and mind? Since we find her either sitting or kneeling at Jesus' feet in all three stories, we can assume she cared deeply for him and was devoted to him and his mission. Though she didn't know the details of what would happen to Jesus, how her heart must have ached knowing the end was near for him.

Even being in a private home, Jesus could not escape the crowds of people for long. They began to congregate around the home. This time, though, they came not just because they wanted to see Jesus, but they also hoped to catch sight of the newest celebrity, Lazarus, the one Jesus brought back from the dead. The religious authorities noticed that, and they decided they needed to have Lazarus put to death also. They wanted to quell any thoughts in people's minds that Jesus raising Lazarus to life again was an indicator he was the Messiah, the one who promised to usher in a new kingdom.

In that moment if we could have seen into the realm where angels and demons exist, we probably would have seen something both amazing and terrifying. Perhaps we would have seen a great struggle between two sets of powers: the powers of evil and darkness and those of love and light. The powers of evil shortsightedly believed by eliminating Jesus they could interrupt God's plans for the salvation of the world. They believed his death would render him powerless. The powers of love and light, though, knew Jesus' death would have the opposite result. It was an essential part of God's great plan to redeem humanity, conquer death, and create a bridge between heaven and earth.

And the next day just as the celebration of Passover began, it was the beginning of the end for Jesus, or so the Chief Priests and Pharisees thought.

When have you sat at Jesus' feet and poured out your love for him?

WHAT CAN WE LEARN FROM THESE STORIES?

Jesus enjoyed spending time with his friends. He also counts each of us as friends and loves spending time with us.

Martha had a lot on her "to do" list that day when she invited Jesus and his companions for dinner. But Jesus preferred simply spending quality time with his friends than having his friends do something to serve him.

He knows many of us are like Martha. We spend much of our lives caught up in the busyness of our world and all we want to accomplish. Sometimes what's on our "to do" lists are even things we do to serve God. But what Jesus wants most for us is to enjoy fellowship with him. Just like he saw it as a delight to spend time with his dear friends, he also welcomes us and delights in spending time with us.

It may be hard for you to believe that Jesus loves spending time with you. What lies might get in the way of believing Jesus really does enjoy time with you?
How does the idea of Jesus enjoying you make you feel?

Jesus recognized Mary and Martha had different gifts, yet he valued what each one gave. He also has given gifts to each of us. Our gifts are the ways his Spirit flows through us, bringing his love, light, and truth into today's world.

While both sisters had gifts of faith and giving, they also had other gifts different from each other. Martha was gifted in hospitality, organization, and leadership. Those gifts were most evident when the "wise, strong, compassionate part" of herself was active rather than the "stressed, bossy, reactive part" of herself. Jesus recognized Martha was a "take charge" kind of woman, and he was okay with that. But he also knew that aspect of her would be used best if it came under God's leadership.

Mary was a contemplative woman with gifts of mercy, discernment, and prophecy. Jesus likely loved her courage in stepping outside of societal expectations for women as she sat at his feet to learn from him. His heart was surely touched by her sacrificial gift to him.

We also are gifted spiritually. God wants to do something in the world through each of us using those gifts. One of the ways He does that is by taking the gifts and talents we've been given and infusing them with His Spirit so we can be a channel through which His spirit flows to a world in need.

All believers have spiritual gifts. What ones are operative in your life as you walk with Jesus?

Jesus understood Martha's frustrations and the negative assumptions she made about her sister. He wasn't offended by it, but he still gently called her out on her judgements of Mary. He does the same for us.

Martha made inaccurate assumptions about what Mary's behavior meant. She likely thought Mary was being lazy, irresponsible, and undependable. She interrupted Jesus' teaching to accuse her sister of leaving her with all the work. Jesus didn't deny the value in Martha's serving but he recognized she was making up a story in her mind about the meaning of Mary's actions. He knew the real reason Mary was sitting at his feet, listening. He understood she had a hunger and thirst in her soul to know more about the Kingdom of God.

Mary may have realized the eternal significance of Jesus' life on earth and how that would impact the future. Martha's thoughts, however, were focused on the present and the practical. Her wrong interpretation of Mary's actions prompted her to ruminate about it and then feel impatient and angry with Mary. As a result, Martha initially missed out on blessings offered to both sisters.

Jesus understands we easily make assumptions that may or may not be accurate about what someone means by their words or actions. Those assumptions then impact our thoughts and feelings, sometimes negatively. He cares about our feelings and doesn't lose patience with us when we misinterpret things. But he wants to help us to learn to sort through and express our emotions in a more constructive way than Martha did.

Have you ever made inaccurate assumptions about someone's actions or words and then became emotionally upset? Or has someone ever made wrong assumptions about something you said or did, and then became upset with you? How did that affect you and the relationship?

When the sisters met Jesus on the road as he came into Bethany, he was not put off by their emotions nor their questioning of him. He came into the middle of their pain rather than remaining outside of it. Jesus is not put off by our questions and emotions, either. He lovingly comes into the middle of our pain to be with us when we invite him.

When faced with the agonizing experience of their brother dying, both sisters wondered why Jesus didn't respond to their request for help. They likely felt raw, human emotions of disappointment, confusion, and maybe anger, along with their grief. But they never lost sight of his healing power nor of their love for Jesus. He listened and cared about what they were going through, and he willingly entered into their pain.

We each experience agony in our life at times, too. Any number of experiences could bring up legitimately strong emotions in us.

Grief is expressed in different ways, sometimes through hurt and sadness, sometimes in anger and doubt. Jesus is never put off when we express our real feelings, and he cares about what we are going through. He wants to be invited into the middle of our pain, hold our hand, put his arm around us, or even hold us as his little child.

When was a time you felt deep sadness, grief, or pain? Where is Jesus in the middle of that pain now?

Mary models for us what it's like to have a surrendered heart.

As Jesus faced what he knew would be excruciating suffering and crucifixion, his heart was deeply moved by Mary's sacrificial generosity and loving ministry to him. Jesus discerned that her heart and soul were entirely yielded to him as the Lord of her life.

What would it be like for you to have a heart surrendered to Jesus in the same way?

PRAYER

Thank you, Jesus, that you love spending time with each of us. Many of us are so busy trying to get through life that we miss out on the blessing of just being with you. Please give us a thirst for more time *being with* you. Teach us what it means to just *be*. Please open moments when there is no need to accomplish something. No clock to watch. No goals to attain. Just. Be. With. You.

Lord, you have gifted each of us in beautiful ways…ways we get to be your hands and feet, eyes and ears, heart, mind, and voice to a hurting and often unloving world. Thank you that your Spirit resides in each of us and flows through us to manifest your love and truth on earth. Please show us more of how you want to work through each of us.

Jesus, we make assumptions everyday about what people mean by their actions and words. Sometimes those assumptions are accurate and sometimes they're not. Misunderstandings contribute to much hurt and conflict between people and groups. This gets played out in our personal lives as well as in the public domain. Please give us the humility needed to question our assumptions, check out their accuracy, and acknowledge when we make a mistaken interpretation of what something means.

Thank you for not being put off by our questions and for your willingness to help us find answers. You accept us when we are emotional, but you want to empower us to use those emotions in a beneficial way. So, Lord, please show us how to do that.

And Lord, you are so worthy of our surrendered hearts and minds!

QUESTIONS FOR PERSONAL REFLECTION AND GROUP SHARING

1. What glimpses of the heart, mind, and character of Jesus do you see in these stories?
2. What do you know about the way God's Spirit most wants to work through you? What is your understanding of your spiritual gifts?
3. What patterns of "making assumptions" do you see in your life? How does that impact your relationships?
4. What was it like for you answering the questions that followed each scenario?

AN EXERCISE TO TRY

We make assumptions or interpretations every day about what someone intends to convey through their actions and words. Sometimes they're based on reality but sometimes they're just a story we make up in our mind about what someone did or said. The problem is when our assumptions don't match what the other person really meant with their words or actions, which often leads to conflict. When we step back and ask ourselves some questions, we interrupt possible conflict before it gets upsetting. When you notice yourself getting upset and starting to assume something negative about someone, step back and ask yourself the following questions. You may find it helpful to journal your answers:

1. "What am I telling myself about that? Could I be making up a story in my mind?"
2. "What are the facts and nothing but the facts about this?"
3. "What negative assumptions or interpretations am I making about myself, another person, or a group?"
4. "What could be other ways of looking at that?" List as many possible explanations as you can. Notice how different you feel when you explore other logical reasons why someone might have done or said something that upset you.
5. Check out your assumptions with the other person to see if what you thought was happening actually matches what they meant.

EIGHT
A Disregarded Woman

MATTHEW 27:55-61; 28:1-8; MARK
15:40-41; 16:1-10; LUKE 8:1-3, 23:49-56
AND 24:1-12; JOHN 19:25-27; 20:1-18

HAVE you ever read a mystery novel, or watched a suspenseful movie, and looked forward to the conclusion when all the loose ends would finally come together? Isn't it satisfying to be able to say, "Oh, wow, how did I not see that happening?"

But have you ever reached the end, and the story remained open-ended, the mystery not fully solved? You were left with, "So...what's the rest of the story?" How dissatisfying is that?

The story of Mary Magdalene is like that. She remains a mystery even today. We don't know how, when, or where Mary met Jesus, yet she traveled with him and his disciples. She was involved in and financially supportive of his ministry. She played a significant role in the story of the crucifixion as she remained at the cross during that traumatic event. Mary was also present on that glorious day of resurrection, continuing to affirm her love for and loyalty to Jesus, her teacher, mentor, and friend. Finally, Jesus entrusted Mary with a message to the disciples.

Because so little is recorded about Mary Magdalene in the New Testament we are left with questions like, "What was Mary's story? How did she become part of Jesus' support team?

What was their relationship like? Where did she go and what did she do after Jesus returned to Heaven?"

Books and movies about Mary Magdalene have captured the public's attention with much fanfare, but there is little information about her or her relationship with Jesus. Perhaps that's how legends developed about her. So, before we talk about what scripture says about Mary, let's talk about two legends surrounding her:

Legend 1: Mary was a former prostitute, a promiscuous but repentant woman.

It's believed she grew up in a fishing village called Magdala (hence, the name Mary of Magdala, or Mary Magdalene) in Northern Israel on the west coast of the Sea of Galilee. As the wealthiest town in that area, it also had a reputation for being a place of immorality. Perhaps that fueled the first legend about Mary.[1]

The legend began around 591 A.D. in a sermon preached by Pope Gregory the First. He taught that Mary Magdalene, Mary of Bethany, and the unnamed "sinful" woman in Luke 7:36-50, were all one woman. Though there is nothing in the Greek translation of the New Testament indicating any truth to this, once the Pope preached this message that story became accepted as true by many.[2] By the 18th century the legend had become so deeply entrenched in what churches taught, both Protestant and Catholic, that many Magdalene Asylums (also called Magdalene Laundries) were opened in Europe, Canada, Australia, and America. They ostensibly were to help women leave a life of prostitution and enter more respectable jobs. In reality they were places where women who'd violated the moral laws were required to do unpaid work as penance for their sins.[3] By the way, the Eastern Orthodox tradition did not view Mary this way; only the Western church did.[4]

That legend about Mary remained intact until 1969 when

Pope Paul VI formally declared the three women were not the same person and Mary Magdalene had not been a prostitute.[5] Finally, in 2016, Pope Francis gave recognition of the valuable role Mary played in Jesus' life and ministry when he affirmed her as the "Apostle to the Apostles." He argued that all four gospels concur she was at the tomb on resurrection day, she was the first person to whom Jesus appeared after he rose from the grave (whether individually or in a group), and Jesus sent Mary to the disciples to give them an important message.[6] Despite these efforts to correct this legend it's still believed by many people today.

Legend 2: Mary and Jesus were married to each other.

This legend is quite controversial! Some Bible teachers believe a Rabbi or teacher in Jesus' day would've had to marry to have credibility. They assume Jesus must have been married and probably to Mary.[7] Here are three clues that dispute that:

First, the New Testament refers to her by naming her hometown rather than her husband. If she were married to Jesus, she would have been referred to as "Mary, the wife of Jesus," instead of "Mary of Magdala."

Second, in John 19:25-27 we read that while Jesus hung on the cross, he saw his mother nearby with her sister, his disciple John (who apparently had not gone into hiding as the other disciples had), and Mary Magdalene. Though Jesus was exhausted and in tremendous pain he still provided for his mother.

"Dear woman, here is your son," Jesus said to his mother as he acknowledged John's presence.

He also said to John, "Here is your mother." From that time on John took Jesus' mother into his home and cared for her. Jesus understood the difficulties a woman could face if she became widowed. With his teachings and his care for his mother's wellbeing as a widow, it's logical he would've also provided for Mary if they'd been married, since his death would've made her a widow.

Third, when Mary met Jesus on Resurrection Day, she addressed him as Rabbouni, an Aramaic term meaning teacher or master. If they had been married, she most likely would've called him by his name or title, or by the Greek word, "aner," meaning "a male human being," or the Hebrew word, "ish" meaning "man."[8]

Much interest in this topic has been fueled in recent years by such media offerings as Dan Brown's book, *The Da Vinci Code*; the movie, *The Last Temptation of Christ*; and Mary's song in the Andrew Lloyd Webber musical, "Jesus Christ Super Star." Despite conjecture about these legends, nothing in the Gospels indicates they are true. So, we will assume they are myths. But Scripture does give us five pieces of information about Mary. Let's explore each one:

First, we know Mary Magdalene was part of a group of women who traveled with Jesus and his disciples and helped to support his ministry financially.

In scripture (Matthew 27:55; Mark 15:40-41; Luke 8:1-3; Luke 23:49) some of these women are named: Mary Magdalene; Mary, the mother of James and Joseph; the mother of the sons of Zebedee; Salome; Joanna, the wife of Herod's steward, Chuza; Susanna; and many others who are unnamed. Knowing that only deepens the mystery about Mary Magdalene and leads us to other questions:

How extensively did the women travel with Jesus? In Matthew 27:55-56 and Mark 15:40-41, we're told the women followed Jesus in the territory of Galilee. But the fact that many were present at the crucifixion indicates they also accompanied him to Jerusalem, located in the territory of Judea.

The significance of this is astounding! It means these women were present in many of the stories we read in the gospels about Jesus although only the twelve male disciples are mentioned in almost all of them.

Why is there so little information given to us about the role these women played in Jesus' ministry? Scripture tells us almost nothing about them. That's not surprising, though, because the culture of Jesus' day devalued women. In most instances women were disqualified from testifying in court because they were viewed as unreliable.[9] Writers of the New Testament would have only emphasized what roles the twelve male disciples played in Jesus' ministry. Despite the apparently significant role women had in Jesus' ministry there are just two verses at the end of Matthew (27:55-56), two at the end of Mark (15:40-41), and four verses in Luke (8:1-3 and 23:49) that even mention the women.

Was it just an afterthought to say women supported Jesus' ministry and traveled with him? Perhaps it was not an intentional disregard but rather, reflective of the accepted but unexamined beliefs of that day about the value of women.

Or is it possible it was intentional? The writers of the gospels wanted their stories about Jesus and his teachings to be accepted by their readers. Perhaps it would've been harder for that message to be believed if there was an emphasis on the part women played in Jesus' ministry. Maybe they believed their readers would see it that way, so they left out details about the women who followed Jesus.

Second, we know Jesus released Mary Magdalene from the power of seven demons. (Mark 16:9.)

We're told nothing of when or how that happened. Had she seen him heal people and decided to seek healing for herself? Or maybe Jesus sensed the anguish within her and reached out to her. No doubt Mary was suffering mentally, emotionally, physically, and spiritually when she first met Jesus.

So, what do we know about demons today? That's another

controversial topic. There are churches where demonic influence is given much attention and some that never mention it. Here are three things we learn about demons from scripture:

First, Scripture says they're real. There are stories in the New Testament that describe Jesus requiring a demon to leave someone. (Matthew 8:28-33; Matthew 17:18; Mark 1:23-27; Mark 3:10-12; Mark: 5:2-20; Mark 7:24-30; Luke 4:33-36 and 40-41; Luke 8:26-39).

What are demons? Christian tradition holds that at one time they were angels who rebelled against God and were banished from heaven (Revelations 12:7-17). Think of them as supernatural beings or entities or forces of evil invested in sowing seeds of anxiety, fear, shame, depression, anger, hatred, bigotry, greed, dishonesty, and injustice to interfere with the Kingdom of God being manifested on earth. Wherever you see actions and attitudes that originate out of greed and self-serving, resentment and hatred, unforgiveness and a need for revenge, dishonesty and cheating others, then some force of evil is helping to facilitate that. You might see it in a terrorist group, in a big corporation, in politics, or even in a church. Basically, demons seek to influence someone to not be aligned with God's plan of bringing His love, mercy, grace, peace, and truth into this world to set people free.

Second, demons don't have as much power as was attributed to them in Jesus' day. Nothing was known about mental or physical illness from a scientific perspective then. The New Testament writers wrote from the context of their cultural understanding. No explanation other than "demonic" would've been given for the mental health diagnoses we call Post Traumatic Stress Disorder, Bipolar Disorder, or panic attacks, or for medical diagnoses, such as Epilepsy, Parkinson's, Rheumatoid Arthritis, or Glaucoma causing blindness.

*Third, w*hen we have experiences that harm us and prompt us to believe things that don't match God's perspective, it's believed demons can attach to our beliefs. Dr. Ed Smith,

Pastoral Counselor, and the developer of Transformation Prayer Ministry (formerly known as Theophostic) teaches, "... Satan launches 'fiery arrows' in our direction (Ephesians 6:16). But it is important to understand both *what* the enemy is targeting and *why* his strategies are so effective. Contrary to popular opinion, the devil does not have us in his sights, for he cannot even touch us (I John 5:18). Why would he waste his arrows by shooting at a target that he cannot hit? He is aiming for what we believe. Specifically, he shoots at the lie-based impurities in our faith. The enemy understands that we feel what we believe, so he targets our impure faith hoping to stir up some emotional pain. These deceptive darts are specifically tailored to your personal set of beliefs."[10] In other words, demons can attach to the negative things we believe about ourselves, other people, and about God, and they actively work to keep us believing those lies.

The people I've worked with in therapy who experienced something truly demonic in their lives were often people who'd endured trauma as a child: abuse, abandonment, rejection, or betrayal. They often didn't feel safe, valued, or loved. Others had become heavily involved in an addiction. Still others nursed feelings of anger, bitterness, or hatred toward themselves or others. On rare occasions if someone had been involved in Satanic worship, whether by their own choice or it was forced on them, they may have acquiesced to demonic influence in their life.

We don't know what happened in Mary Magdalene's life prior to her first encounter with Jesus. Did she experience the presence of seven entities? Did she suffer from a mental health condition? Had she experienced trauma that prompted her to believe lies to which demonic power had attached? Or did she experience a combination of that? We don't know. Whatever it was, Mary likely was suffering from depression, anxiety, fear, shame, guilt, or anger when she met Jesus.

Can you imagine what it was like for Mary to suddenly be

freed by Jesus from the influence of demons? I've had people tell me when someone says to a demon, "Stop, be quiet in the name of Jesus Christ," suddenly all the noise and chaos in their mind stopped. While we don't know how or when it happened, we know Jesus released Mary from all that. He quieted the self-condemnation circling round in her mind, filled the emptiness in her heart, calmed the restlessness in her spirit, and set her free to embrace her truest identity as a precious, deeply loved child of God.

None of us made it to adulthood without some painful happenings that negatively affected us. Some of us came to believe "lies" as, "I'm responsible for taking care of everyone and everything." "I have to be perfect." "My needs aren't important." "I don't deserve love." These things *feel* true, but they are lies because they don't represent how God thinks or feels about us. Demons are invested in keeping us believing those lies. And sometimes demonic influence is so subtle we would never know it is present.

Why would this occur? The Evil One wants to interfere with us being fully free to allow God's Spirit to do whatever He wants to do within us and through us. They want to block God's mercy, grace, and love from being shared. Demons also want to interfere with our sense of being acceptable, lovable, and purposeful.

The third piece of information we know about Mary is she was a loving support throughout Jesus' ministry but also during the most agonizing moments of his life. She was one of the few people courageous enough to stay with him to the end of his horrific ordeal at the cross.

In Matthew 27:55, Mark 15:40, and in John 19:25, we read Mary stood near the cross as Jesus was crucified. How agonizing it must've been to hear the pounding of the spikes driven through his flesh into those wooden beams, to see the deep, bloody cuts from the brutal flogging, and to taste the salt from her tears. Yet, she stayed. She didn't run away or hide. She probably felt very scared, but she didn't allow her fear to interfere with being a support and an expression of love to Jesus. Undoubtedly, he could see her as he hung on that cross. It must have comforted him to know she was present and offered comfort to his mother. She even followed Joseph of Arimathea as he placed Jesus' body in a tomb. (The disciples had good reason to hide at this time. Rome often executed the followers in a movement the same way they executed the leader.)

Fourth, we learn Mary was the first person, whether in a group or individually, to whom Jesus appeared on that momentous Resurrection Day.

Before sunrise on the first day of the week Mary went to the tomb to anoint Jesus' body with the customary spices. And *here* is where the mystery deepens because there are five versions of what took place that morning, depending on which Gospel you read (Mark had two different versions).

In Matthew, Mark (first of his two versions), and Luke, Mary was not alone as she went to the tomb, but she was alone in Mark (second version) and John's gospel. Angels greeted the women in Matthew, Mark (first version), Luke, and John. Jesus greeted the women in Matthew, Mark (second version) and John. The women were instructed to go tell the disciples that Jesus had risen and to meet him in Galilee (about forty miles from Jerusalem) in Matthew and Mark. But in John, Jesus gave a different message to Mary to convey to the disciples. In Mark (second version) and Luke, the disciples thought the women were talking nonsense when they shared that Jesus had risen from death. In Luke and John, one or two disciples came out of hiding and went to the tomb to check out the women's story.

Finally, Jesus commissioned Mary to take an important message to his disciples.

In John's version of Resurrection Day, Mary went to the tomb alone before sunrise. Maybe she couldn't sleep due to nightmares and flashbacks of the recent horrific events. Perhaps she decided to just get up and go to the tomb to complete the job they hadn't finished because of the start of the Sabbath. Though Jesus had told his followers he would die but then be resurrected on the third day, the trauma Mary had witnessed had been so raw, so graphic that it likely seemed impossible. Maybe she even forgot Jesus' words. As she made her way to the tomb, she had no idea she was going to be a witness to the first Easter. How surprised she was to see the stone moved! She hurriedly ran to where the disciples were hiding.

"They've taken the Lord out of the tomb, and we don't know where they have put him," she exclaimed (John 20:2). Peter and another disciple, likely John, raced to the tomb to see for themselves if Mary's story was true. Mary followed. When they arrived, the men stepped inside and saw the empty grave clothes lying there. They were amazed but soon returned to the other disciples.

Mary remained alone at the tomb after the two disciples left. Still convinced Jesus was dead, crying, and distraught, she peeked into the tomb and saw two angels seated where Jesus' head and feet had laid.

"Woman, why are you crying?" they asked her. (John 20:13)

"They've taken my Lord away and I don't know where they put him," she replied (John 20:13).

She turned to leave and that was when she saw Jesus. She didn't recognize him, though. Perhaps she struggled to focus through her tears and the early dawn light. Or maybe the trauma of it all still echoed in her mind so loudly that the reality of Jesus standing in front of her didn't seem even remotely possible.

"Woman, why are you crying? Who is it you are looking for?" Jesus asked. (John 20:15)

Thinking he was the gardener, she answered, "Sir, if you have carried him away, tell me where you have laid him, and I will take him away."(John 20:15)

When he called out her name, "Mary," she immediately recognized his voice.

"Rabbouni!" she exclaimed.

Suddenly her sadness was gone. "He's alive!" must have reverberated through her heart, mind, and body. What joy!

If someone you loved unexpectedly showed up would your first response be to rush to give them a big hug? Apparently, that was Mary's response. But Jesus told her not to hold onto him because he had not yet ascended into heaven.

Maybe you're wondering, "Why did he not want her to touch him?" Perhaps Jesus responded to her like that because, as they stood face to face, they interacted from different planes of reality. Mary was still in the realm of earth in which the Kingdom of God was "the now and the not yet." Jesus was already in the realm of eternity where the Kingdom of God was fully present.

Then Jesus said to Mary, "Go to my brothers and say to them, 'I am returning to my Father and your Father, to my God and your God.'" (John 20:17)

The significance of this is phenomenal for Mary as well as for all of us!

First and foremost, Jesus' resurrection means he was more powerful than all the powers that tried to wipe him out. He did what he came to earth to do. He defeated death. And with that he provided a way for all of us to connect with God, the Father. He became the way to freedom from sin and brokenness and to abundant life. Now it was time for him to return to his Father in Heaven.

Second, in John's version of the resurrection, the first person to whom Jesus appeared was a woman. He could easily have appeared to Peter and the other disciple, but he did not. He could have simply given his message to Peter and asked him to deliver it to the other disciples, but again, he did not. He would've known Peter and the other disciple arrived at the tomb but apparently, Jesus waited until they were gone before he appeared to Mary.

Third, in John's version, it wasn't just a simple, practical message of, "Tell them to meet me in Galilee." It essentially meant, "I am going back to my Father and my God who is also your Father and God." Consider the significance of that. Jesus wanted his disciples to know they had the same Father and God he had, even though they deserted him and were in hiding. Jesus asked Mary to take that message to them. He chose her to be his messenger. And since being a messenger of God and sharing the gospel is the definition of an "apostle," in the words of Pope Francis, it seems Jesus commissioned Mary to be an "Apostle to the Apostles.[11]

If you consider the value women had back then, everything suddenly shifted that day. Though the culture viewed them as second-class, it became clear women were highly valued by Jesus. He apparently saw them as trusted and reliable, someone given gifts. Those gifts included leadership gifts and voices to speak, even if the culture back then did not recognize that shift.

Mary left that encounter with Jesus and delivered the message to the disciples Jesus asked her to share. But that was just the beginning of the adventure God planned for her. She never went back to her old life. Instead, she spent the rest of her life ministering in Jesus' name and sharing the Good News of the Gospel as the Spirit empowered her.

Despite being disregarded as a woman, we know Mary Magdalene's life was completely changed by Jesus. When he removed seven demons from her, she was set free from the desperate depression, anxiety, and shame that may have held her captive. She was healed of the negative impact of whatever traumas she had experienced in her life. She was also set free from the power of the lies she believed about herself, others, and God.

That initial healing by Jesus was then deepened as she daily opened her heart and mind to his teachings. She allowed his love to shine its light into the darkest places of pain within her. She also granted residence to Jesus to all the rooms of her heart and mind. As a result, his love, mercy, grace, peace, truth, and wisdom were expressed through her.

Mary Magdalene was healed and transformed by Jesus. She went from being very troubled to being at peace. She became a woman of courage, wisdom, strength, compassion, and vision. She couldn't have imagined becoming a leader, yet God used her in that way throughout the rest of her life. Her legacy remains to this day. She demonstrates what the life changing power of Jesus can do when he is given the opportunity to work in a woman's life: forgiving her sin, setting her free from what pain and lies have held her back, filling her with His Spirit, and empowering her to share the love of God with the world.

WHAT CAN WE LEARN FROM MARY'S STORY?

Jesus saw, heard, and truly understood Mary. He knew her failures and sin but also the real person underneath her pain and brokenness. He knows all that about each of us too.

He didn't judge Mary. He understood how her life had been impacted by painful things that happened to her as well as choices she'd made. He knew how much she suffered. Though Mary likely was tormented and despairing when they first met, Jesus recognized Mary's truest self behind her emotions and any troubled behavior she displayed.

Jesus also sees our pain. He knows and cares about any sadness and depression, anxiety and fear, embarrassment and shame, and anger and resentment we sometimes experience. He doesn't look down on us for that. He knows and cares about the painful things we're currently going through and what we have experienced in the past. He knows how we have been sinned against and how we have sinned. He still accepts and loves us. He is not thrown off, put off, or turned off by any of our unhealthy behavior or thoughts. He longs to show us a better way, but he patiently waits for us to be ready to allow him to lead us. The beautiful potential with which each of us has been designed is also known and valued by Jesus. He loves it when we allow him to free us to live out of that potential.

What feelings of depression, anxiety, shame, or anger are you experiencing?
How does that affect your freedom to live how God wants you to live?
What do you believe about the potential you have within you?

Jesus believed in Mary's value as a woman and in her ability to deliver a message. He also sees us the same way.

He knew because she was a woman, others would disregard Mary, but he still trusted her reliability. He believed in her ability and willingness to take his message to the group of men who followed him. Jesus knew he could count on her to do whatever he asked of her. No doubt, her history with mental illness and demonic infection gave her a unique ability to compassionately understand those who believed their situation was hopeless. It allowed her to minister more effectively in His name. Jesus also saw beyond any kind of negative cultural beliefs about women, and he was not hesitant to empower Mary to live outside them.

Jesus knows and understands the ways we may have been disregarded or held back in life. He also understands what biases others might have had against us. He knows the doors that may have been closed to us. Even if those things have happened in our lives, he knows the full value of each of us.

What doors have been closed to you in your life, and how did that affect you?
How have you been disregarded?
What is the truth Jesus wants you to know about yourself?

Mary was not too "messed up" for God to use her in building His kingdom here on earth, and you aren't either.

How much does depression interfere with you having the energy and motivation to do things you'd love to do in your life? Or does anxiety hold you back from following what you believe God's Spirit wants to do within and through you? How is your sense of worth defined by the mistakes you've made, your comparison of yourself to others, or by someone else's negative judgements of you? If you've ever found yourself in any of these scenarios it wouldn't be surprising. Not only has every woman I've worked with in therapy experienced them on occasion but so has every woman I've known, including myself.

We've all had times of doubting ourselves or disbelieving we mattered. Many of us have felt we did not belong. Some have wondered how God could possibly use us because we are "imperfect," or "not enough," or "just too much." We've all believed lies about ourselves at times, but we don't want anyone to know that. So, we try to hide them and hope nobody discovers those things we dislike about ourselves. If the negative feelings get triggered, we then engage in behaviors to try to cover up or distract us from feeling that way.

If these are things you're feeling, you aren't alone. In today's world both anxiety and depression affect the lives of many women. According to the National Institute of Mental Health, 23.4 percent of women have an anxiety diagnosis.[12] However, that number doesn't count numerous others whose lives border on the edges of anxiety, constantly feeling they have too much to do and too little time or resources to do it, who worry about making mistakes or upsetting someone.

Depression among women has continued to rise. In 2025, the Gallup National Health and Well-Being Index indicated 23.4 percent of women are being treated for depression, up from 17.6 percent in 2017. But women aged 18-29 years experienced the greatest increase in depression, moving up from 13 percent in 2017 to 26.7 percent in 2025.[13] According to the World Health Organization, about 6.9 percent of women worldwide have a depression diagnosis.[14] These numbers don't include women who experience low-grade depression but don't have enough symptoms to receive an official diagnosis that allows them to get help.

Anxiety and depression are rampant but also complicated. When I became a therapist many years ago, I was taught there were primarily three reasons why someone would be anxious or depressed: (A.) An imbalance in the neurotransmitters in the brain, and the recommended treatment was to take medication; (B.) Something called, "Stinkin' thinkin'," which meant someone engaged in pessimistic and critical thought patterns. Cognitive Therapy was recommended to help change those patterns. (C.) Unresolved trauma from childhood which often meant doing "talk therapy," sometimes for years. Of course, from a spiritual perspective, anxiety and depression were often seen as "not trusting God enough." The recommendation was for a woman to read her Bible and pray more. While these are all valuable tools, they don't address all the reasons someone could be anxious or depressed.

During my years in the mental health field, what I observed is that some people felt better after they went on a mild anti-anxiety or anti-depressant medication, while that didn't help others. Some found relief in learning how to change their thought patterns and speak to themselves in a kinder, more compassionate, encouraging way, while understanding how to do that was elusive to others. Some felt much better when they released the negative impact of past trauma from their mind and body through such therapies as EMDR (Eye Movement Desensitization and Reprocessing) and EFT (Emotional Freedom Technique), which I've mentioned in previous chapters, but some did not.

Still others never felt better until it was finally discovered they had an undiagnosed medical problem, such as having Lyme Disease, an overgrowth of Candida, parasites in the blood, or mold growing in their body. Dr. Chris Mote of Cornerstone Health Community in Colorado says, "Candida is like two 12-year-olds at Halloween with a box of eggs and toilet paper, it's gonna be a mess to clean up. Mold is like a gang with weapons and they can break in and hurt you."[15] And spiritually, some people experienced spontaneous, miraculous healing in response to prayer, but some didn't.

I began to keep a list of factors contributing to the depression and anxiety my clients experienced. That list now includes fifty factors. A diagram I created about that is on my website. If you are experiencing depression or anxiety that doesn't seem to go away, and if it's not made better by more Bible study, prayer, being in community with others, taking medication, and even doing therapy, it's possible you have something else going on in your mind or body.

Look through the diagram to see if there might be other factors that could contribute to what you feel. If you think there could be something physiologically contributing to anxiety or depression, talk to your primary care physician, or contact a Functional Medicine doctor who will explore the reasons behind the symptoms, not just treat the symptoms. If you have past trauma you've never dealt with, I encourage you to connect with a Christian therapist trained in EMDR or a Spiritual Director who does Immanuel Prayer.

If you've been depressed, anxious, or have any other chronic emotional or physical difficulty, you haven't been forgotten. Jesus knows and cares about what you are going through. It might not be a quick and effortless process, but he wants to bring you to a place of peace like he did for Mary Magdalene. And just like he blessed the world through Mary, he wants to do that through you also.

PRAYER

Lord, Jesus, you know there is a Mary Magdalene inside each of us. Someone who has been sinned against. Someone who has sinned. But also, someone designed by you in a beautiful way for a purpose. We've each had times of going away from our truest self and some of us, like Mary, have never even known our truest self because of life's difficulties. Please show us who we really are in your eyes. Help us begin to see ourselves with the same kind of love and tenderness you have for us.

You know the tumultuous emotions many of us feel of depression, anxiety, or anger. Even though we hate feeling that way and often feel shame about it, you still accept us and long to be invited into all of that. God, for any who identify with that, please reveal your acceptance and deep love to us in such a concrete, tangible way that we cannot miss it. Let that love go down deep to any place inside where pain resides. Set us free from pain and shame's power.

Please strengthen us as we examine what "lies" feel true to us today about ourselves, other people, or you. Give us your grace and strength to face whatever memories are the origins of those lies. Give us awareness of your presence being with us in that. Set us free from the power of the lies we believe. Replace them with your truth about who we really are as your cherished child.

Set us free to live an abundant life. Even if we think it's too late. Even if doors have been closed to us. Please give us your wisdom, strength, and a vision for what you want to do *in* us, *with* us, and *through* us. Transform us and fill us with your Spirit, just as you did for Mary Magdalene. May we experience a sense of being blessed and then empowered to be a blessing to others.

QUESTIONS FOR PERSONAL REFLECTION AND GROUP SHARING

1. What glimpses of the heart, mind, and character of Jesus do you see in these stories about Mary Magdalene?
2. What are ways you identify with Mary Magdalene?
3. Mary was accused of being a former prostitute and a promiscuous but repentant woman. We now know these things are not true about her. Has there ever been a time when you were accused of something that was not true? What happened and how did that impact your life?
4. If you've ever been in a situation in which you devoted time and energy to something but later, someone else was given credit for it and you were disregarded, what happened and how did that affect you?
5. If you've ever had doors closed to you because you were a woman, what happened and how did that impact your life?
6. What lies did you come to believe about yourself, others, or about God in those situations? What does God say about that?
7. What does God want to do in your life, so you no longer live with leftover pain or lies?

TWO EXERCISES TO TRY

1. Read the first four books of the New Testament from a different perspective. As you read the stories about Jesus and his twelve disciples, hold a picture in your mind of women being present in those stories. Think about what it might have been like for the women to travel throughout Galilee and some of Judea. Perhaps they also traveled through Samaria with Jesus and the twelve disciples. Notice what thoughts and feelings you have as you read from that perspective.

2. We've all heard messages about the Resurrection on Easter Sunday, but usually the teaching comes from only one of the Gospels. Try reading the story from all four gospels and note the differences. Each gospel offers a different perspective.

Resources

The following resources can give you more information about the topics covered in this book.

BOOKS:

Amen, Dr. Daniel. *Change Your Brain, Change Your Life*, Harmony Books, 1998 and 2015.

Allen, Jennie. *Get Out of Your Head: Stopping the Spiral Toxic Thoughts*, Waterbrook, 2020.

Allender, Dan. *The Wounded Heart: Hope for Adult Victims of Childhood Sexual Abuse*, Nav Press, 2018.

Bernhard, Toni. *How to Live Well with Chronic Pain and Illness: A Mindful Guide*, Wisdom Publications, 2014.

Chapman, Gary and Campbell, Ross. *The Five Love Languages of Children,* Northfield Publishing, 1997.

Clinton, Dr. Tim and Sibcy, Dr. Gary. *Attachments: Why You Love, Feel, and Act the Way You Do,* Integrity Publishers, 2002.

Dana, Dr. Deb. *Polyvagal Practices: Anchoring the Self in Safety*, Norton Professional Books, 2023.

Jobson, Dr. Meghan, and Morgan, Dr. Juliet. *Long Illness:*

A Practical Guide to Surviving, Healing, and Thriving, Hachette Books, 2023.

Lake, Dr. Steven. *The Great Adventure: Pursuing God's Specific Purpose for Your Life*, 2022.

Langberg, Diane Mandt, PhD. *Suffering and the Heart of God: How Trauma Destroys and Christ Restores*, New Growth Press, 2015.

Sahyouni, Dr. X Nader. *Anxiety Transformed: Prayer That Brings Enduring Change*, Crossing Place Media, 2022.

Smith, Sherrie Rice, RN. *EFT for Christians*, Energy Psychology Press, 2015.

Smith, Dr. Ed and Joshua Smith. *Transformation Prayer Ministry: Principles, Purposes, Process*, New Creation Publishing, 2023 updated version. (This training is downloadable for free.)

Stack, Debi. *Martha to the Max: Balanced Living for the Perfectionists*, Moody Press, 2000.

Suzuki, Dr. Wendy. *Good Anxiety: Harnessing the Power of the Most Misunderstood Emotion*, Atria, 2021.

Thurman, Dr. Chris. *The Lies We Believe*, Thomas Nelson, 1999.

Warner, Marcus. *Understanding the Wounded Heart*, second edition, Deeper Walk, 2019.

Warren, Rick. *The Purpose Driven Life: What On Earth Am I Here For?*, Zondervan, 2002 and 2012.

Weaver, Joanna. *Having a Mary Heart in a Martha World: Finding Intimacy with God in the Busyness of Life*, Waterbrook, 2002.

Webb, Joan C. *The Relief of Imperfection: For Women Who Try Too Hard to Make It Just Right*, Regal, 2007.

WEBSITES

Please visit my website at **www.vickieatontherapy.com**, where you can get in touch with me. I have a number of free downloads there for you, including:

A. Diagram of Fifty Factors That Contribute to Anxiety and Depression
B. Spiritual Gifts Assessment
C. Purpose Assessment

www.endria.org *Eye Movement Desensitization and Reprocessing, or EMDR* is a kind of psychotherapy that involves bilateral stimulation of the left and right brain. It is an evidence-based therapy that helps someone release the negative emotional charge they still carry from a trauma they experienced. It is particularly helpful when someone experiences symptoms of Post Traumatic Stress Disorder. This website offers a directory of therapists who use EMDR.

www.EFTforChristians.com offers much information about using EFT (Emotional Freedom Technique) for healing.

www.immanuelapproach.com provides a directory of both therapists and lay people trained in facilitating Immanuel Prayer.

www.netgrace.org GRACE (Godly Christian Response to Abuse in the Christian Environment) is a non-profit organization that trains Christian organizations to recognize, respond to sex abuse allegations, and to prevent it from happening.

www.onelifemaps.com offers a series of eight maps that can help you discover and clarify the meaning of your life's story.

www.rainn.org RAINN (Rape, Abuse, and Incest National Network) is a national organization against sexual violence. It operates a National Sexual Assault Hotline, offers programs for sexual violence prevention, is a resource for survivors, and facilitates perpetrators being brought to justice.

www.transformationprayer.org offers a resource for inner healing prayer.

www.theultimatejourney.org Christ Life Ministries, Des Moines, IA offers 3-day "Turbos" in Iowa and 13-week groups. You can receive information about any groups offered near you.

Notes

1. AN OLD WOMAN AND A YOUNG WOMAN

1. See www.enterthebible.org/time-period/judea-during-roman-rule
2. Van Der Kolk, Bessel, *The Body Keeps the Score*, Penguin Book , p. 79-87, and www.webmd.com/mental-health/what-does-fight-flight-freeze-fawn-mean

2. A DESPAIRING WOMAN

1. See www.mayoclinic.org, Von Willebrand's Disease
2. See www.christianlibrary.org, Uncleanness
3. See Leviticus 12:1-8
4. www.cdc.gov, Statistics on Chronic illnesses
5. Schiraldi, Glenn R., *The Post-Traumatic Stress Disorder Handbook*, McGraw-Hill, 2000.
6. Dana, Deb, *Polyvagal Practices: Anchoring the Self in Safety*, Norton Professional Books, 2023, p. 5 - 10.

3. A SCANDALOUS WOMAN

1. See www.gotquestions.org/613-commandments.html
2. Bailey, Kenneth E., *Jesus Through Middle Eastern Eyes*, InterVarsity Press, 2008, p. 242.
3. Ibid, p. 243.
4. Ibid, p. 248.
5. Ibid, p. 243-244.
6. See www.biblehub.com/topical/d/denarius.htm
7. NIV Study Bible, Kenneth Barker (ed). Zondervan, 2020.
8. psychiatryonline.org/doi/10.1176/ajp.155.5.6
9. Luke 7:47, Life Application Bible, NRSV

4. A DESPISED WOMAN

1. McClelland, Kristi, *Jesus and Women: In the First Century and Now*, Lifeway Press, 2019, p. 60-61.
2. See "Divorce After Ten Years Childless," at https://www.outorah.org/p/85815

3. See soencouragement.org/divorce5.htm
4. gotquestions.org/concubine-concubines.html
5. Ortberg, John, *The Life You've Always Wanted*, Zondervan Publishing House, 2006, p. 127.

5. A DISCARDED WOMAN

1. https://jesusalive.cc/how-killed-by-stoning/
2. Bailey, Kenneth E., *Jesus Through Middle Eastern Eyes: Cultural Studies in the Gospels*, Intervarsity Press, 2008, p. 235.
3. www.rainn.org/get-informed/facts-statistics-the-scope-of-the-problem RAINN's statistics were taken from the National Crime Victimization Survey conducted annually by the U.S. Justice Department.
4. https://sojo.net/articles/news/why-so-many-catholic-dioceses-file-bankruptcy
5. www.netgrace.org

6. A DESPERATE WOMAN

1. See footnotes for both passages in the NIV Life Application Study Bible, Zondervan, 2019.

8. A DISREGARDED WOMAN

1. www.biblicalarchaeology.org, "Where Was Mary Magdalene From?"
2. LeLoup, Jean-Yves, *The Gospel of Mary Magdalene*, Inner Traditions International, 2002, preface
3. See https://www.britannica.com/topic/Magdalene-laundry
4. King, Karen. *The Gospel of Mary of Magdala: Jesus and the First Woman Apostle,* Polestar Press, 2003, p.149.
5. www.christianity.com/wiki/people/who-was-mary-magdalene-and-why-do-people-think-she-was-a-prostitute.html
6. See www.futurechurch.org, "Mary Magdalene: An Apostle for Our Times."
7. For a detailed critique by theology professor Mikel Del Rosario, see https://apologeticsguy.com/2019/11/was-jesus-married/E
8. See biblicalgenderroles.com/2021/06/08/there-is-no-word-for-husband-in-the-orginal-language-of-the-bible
9. See www.Jewsforjesus.org/learn/the-role-of-women-in-the-Bible/
10. Smith, Dr. Ed and Joshua Smith, "Transformation Prayer Ministry: Principles, Purposes, Process," New Creation Publishing, 2023 updated version. This training is downloadable for free.
11. www.crossroadsinitiative.com/media/articles/Mary-Magdalene-Apostle to the Apostles.

12. See www.nimh.nih.gov/health/statistics
13. See www.news.gallup.com, Statistics on Depression, May 2025.
14. See https://www.who.int/news-room/fact-sheets/detail/depression
15. From an October 2025 text conversation I had with Dr. Mote.

www.ingramcontent.com/pod-product-compliance
Lightning Source LLC
Chambersburg PA
CBHW070452100426
42743CB00010B/1584